Study Guide

for use with

Intermediate Accounting

Third Edition

Volume II, Chapters 13-22

J. David Spiceland
University of Memphis

James F. Sepe
Santa Clara University

Lawrence A. Tomassini
The Ohio State University

Prepared by
J. David Spiceland
James F. Sepe

 Irwin

Boston   Burr Ridge, IL   Dubuque, IA   Madison, WI   New York   San Francisco   St. Louis
Bangkok   Bogotá   Caracas   Kuala Lumpur   Lisbon   London   Madrid   Mexico City
Milan   Montreal   New Delhi   Santiago   Seoul   Singapore   Sydney   Taipei   Toronto

Study Guide, Volume II, Chapters 13-22 for use with
INTERMEDIATE ACCOUNTING
J. David Spiceland, James F. Sepe, Lawrence A. Tomassini

1 2 3 4 5 6 7 8 9 0 QPD/QPD 0 9 8 7 6 5 4 3

ISBN 0-07-250412-9

www.mhhe.com

The McGraw-Hill Companies

Contents

Current Liabilities and Contingencies

LEARNING OBJECTIVES

After studying this chapter you should be able to:
1. Define liabilities and distinguish between current and long-term liabilities.
2. Account for the issuance and payment of various forms of notes and record the interest on the notes.
3. Characterize accrued liabilities and describe when and how they should be recorded.
4. Determine when a liability can be classified as a noncurrent obligation, including the exceptions to the general classification criteria.
5. Identify situations that constitute contingencies and the circumstances under which they should be accrued.
6. Describe the appropriate accounting treatment for contingencies, including unasserted claims and assessments.

CHAPTER HIGHLIGHTS

PART A: CURRENT LIABILITIES

Three essential characteristics of a liability are identified in the definition provided by Concepts Statement 6. Liabilities:

1. are **probable, future** sacrifices of economic benefits.
2. that arise from **present** obligations (to transfer goods or provide services) to other entities.
3. that result from **past** transactions or events.

In general, liabilities should be recorded at their *present values*. However, liabilities *payable within one year* are exempted from this requirement and may be recorded at their *face values*.

For financial reporting purposes, liabilities are classified as either *current* liabilities or *long-term* liabilities. Current liabilities are those expected to be satisfied with *current assets* or by the creation of other *current liabilities*. Usually (with exceptions), these are obligations payable within one year or within the firm's operating cycle, whichever is longer. Classifying liabilities as either current or long-term assists investors and creditors in assessing the riskiness of a company's obligations.

Current Liabilities and Contingencies

The usual types of current liabilities and related accounting issues are described below:

Accounts Payable and Trade Notes Payable

Accounts payable are obligations to suppliers of goods or services that are used in the production and/or sale of goods and services and are purchased on credit. These liabilities typically are non-interest-bearing. The critical accounting aspects of accounts payable are determining their existence and insuring that they are recorded in the proper accounting period.

Trade notes payable differ from accounts payable in that they are formally recognized by a written note and generally bear interest. Interest is calculated as:

> FACE AMOUNT x ANNUAL RATE x TIME TO MATURITY

Short-Term Notes Payable

Short-term notes payable may also arise from cash borrowings from banks or other financial institutions. Most companies rely heavily on short-term financing. A **line of credit** allows a company to borrow cash without having to follow formal loan procedures and paperwork. The interest may be paid *in addition to* the face amount (interest-bearing note) or *included in* the face amount (noninterest-bearing note).

ILLUSTRATION

INTEREST-BEARING NOTE:

Seattle Metal Works borrowed $400,000 cash under a short-term line of credit arrangement and issued a 4-month, 12% promissory note. Interest was payable at maturity.

To record the issuance of the note:

Cash	400,000	
Notes payable		400,000

To record the payment of the note plus interest:

Interest expense ($400,000 x 12% x $^{4}/_{12}$)	16,000	
Notes payable..	400,000	
Cash ($400,000 + 16,000)..		416,000

NONINTEREST-BEARING NOTE:

Assume the preceding note was packaged as a $400,000 noninterest-bearing note, with a 12% "discount rate." In that case, the $16,000 interest would be "discounted" at the outset.

To record the issuance of the note:

Cash (difference)..	384,000	
Discount on notes payable ($400,000 x 12% x $^{4}/_{12}$])	16,000	
Notes payable (face amount)		400,000

To record the payment of the note plus interest:

Interest expense	16,000	
Discount on notes payable		16,000
Notes payable (face amount)	400,000	
Cash		400,000

When interest is "discounted" from the face amount of a note, the effective interest rate is higher than the stated discount rate because the amount borrowed is only $384,000, but the interest is calculated as the *discount rate* times the $400,000 face amount:

	$ 16,000	interest for 4 months
÷	$384,000	amount borrowed
=	4.167%	rate for 4 months
x	12/4	to annualize the rate
=	12.5%	effective interest rate

Commercial Paper

Commercial paper refers to unsecured notes sold in minimum denominations of $25,000 with maturities ranging from 30 to 270 days. Commercial paper frequently is purchased by other companies as a short-term investment and interest usually is discounted at the issuance of the note. It usually is backed by a line of credit with a bank, allowing the interest rate to be lower than in a bank loan. Accounting for commercial paper is exactly the same as for other short-term notes as shown in our previous illustration.

Accrued Liabilities

Accrued liabilities arise when expenses already have been *incurred*, but cash has not yet been paid (accrued expenses). These are recorded by *adjusting entries* at the end of the reporting period, prior to preparing financial statements.

Examples are: **salaries payable**, **income taxes payable**, and **interest payable**. For illustration, assume salaries of $600,000 have been earned by employees by the end of the period, but will not be paid to employees until the following period. The expense and related liability are recorded as:

Salaries expense..	600,000	
Salaries payable..		600,000

Deposits and Advances from Customers

When cash is received from a customer as a refundable deposit or as an advance payment for products or services, a liability is created to return the deposit or to supply the products or services. For instance, if a utility company collects a deposit when service is begun for a new customer, a liability, say "Liability – refundable deposits," is recorded. Similarly, a magazine publisher records a liability from the sale of magazine subscriptions. The liability, say "Liability – magazine subscriptions," converts to revenue when magazines are mailed.

Like other liabilities, obligations produced by customer deposits and advances are classified as current or long-term liabilities, depending on when the obligation is expected to be satisfied.

Collections for Third Parties

Firms often make collections from customers or from employees on behalf of tax authorities or other third parties. The companies then periodically remit these amounts to the appropriate parties. In the meantime, these amounts represent liabilities. Examples include **sales taxes**, **payroll taxes**, **employee withholding taxes**, **insurance**, and **union dues**.

Current Maturities of Long-Term Debt

A long-term obligation *usually* is **reclassified** as a current liability when it becomes payable (or callable) within the coming year (or operating cycle). For instance, a 30-year note is reported as a long-term liability for 29 years, but is classified as a current liability in its 30th year.

Exception: Short-term obligations can be reported as noncurrent liabilities if the company
(a) *intends* to refinance on a long-term basis and
(b) demonstrates the *ability* to do so by a refinancing agreement or by actual financing.

For instance, if new long-term notes (or bonds or even new stock) will be issued, and the proceeds used to pay the maturity amount of the 30-year notes above, the liability is classified as a long-term liability.

Several weeks usually pass between the end of a company's fiscal year and the date the financial statements are issued. To support a company's ability to refinance on a long-term basis, a refinancing agreement or actual financing can occur after the end of the fiscal year, but must exist prior to the issuance of financial statements. An existing credit agreement with a bank that permits long-term borrowing of a sufficient amount can be used to meet this criterion.

PART B: CONTINGENCIES

A **loss contingency** exists when a potential loss depends on whether some future event occurs (e.g., a pending lawsuit at year-end for which the outcome will not be known until after the financial statements are issued). Whether a contingency is accrued and reported as a liability depends on:

    (a)   the *likelihood* that the confirming event will occur:
1. probable – confirming event is likely to occur
2. reasonably possible– the chance the confirming event will occur is more than remote but less than likely
3. remote– the chance the confirming event will occur is slight

and (b)   what can be determined about the *amount* of loss.
1. known
2. reasonably estimable
3. not reasonably estimable

A contingent liability is recorded if (1) a loss is **probable** (the confirming event is likely to occur) and (2) the amount of loss can be at least **reasonably estimated**.

```
Loss (or expense)..................................................................    x,xxx
        Liability..................................................................................         x,xxx
```

If either of these criteria is **not** met, and if there is at least a **reasonable possibility** that the loss will occur, only **footnote disclosure** should be made.

The possibilities are illustrated below:

DOLLAR AMOUNT OF POTENTIAL LOSS

LIKELIHOOD	Known	Reasonably Estimable	Not Reasonably Estimable
Probable	Liability Accrued & Disclosure Note	Liability Accrued & Disclosure Note	Disclosure Note Only
Reasonably Possible	Disclosure Note Only	Disclosure Note Only	Disclosure Note Only
Remote	No Disclosure Required	No Disclosure Required	No Disclosure Required

                                                                         Intermediate Accounting, 3/e

Most consumer products are accompanied by a warranty or guarantee. **Warranties** and **guarantees** are loss contingencies for which the conditions for accrual almost always are met.

Warranty expense ([3% + 4%] x $2,000,000)	140,000	
Estimated warranty liability		140,000

Thus, we record the costs of satisfying guarantees as expenses in the same accounting period as the revenues from the products sold (matching principle).

Similarly, we also accrue a liability in connection with **premium** offers. Companies frequently offer premium (cash rebates, cents-off coupons, toys for box tops, etc.) to stimulate sales. The cost of premiums estimated to be provided to customers represents an **expense** and an **estimated liability** in the reporting period the product is sold.

Subsequent Events

Recall that several weeks usually pass between the end of a company's fiscal year and the date the financial statements for that year are issued. When the cause of a loss contingency occurs before the year-end, a clarifying event after the year-end but before the financial statements are issued can be used to determine how the contingency is reported.

Unasserted Claims and Assessments

Even if a claim has yet to be made when the financial statements are issued, we still may need to accrue or disclose a contingency. For instance, the EPA may have been investigating a chemical spill by a chemical company but hasn't yet proposed a penalty for violation of environmental laws. Even then, if it is *probable* that an unasserted claim or assessment or an unfiled lawsuit will occur, we apply the usual criteria (probable unfavorable outcome and reasonably estimable amount) to consider whether and how to report the possible loss.

Gain Contingencies

A **gain contingency** (an uncertain situation that might result in a gain) is not accrued. Instead, we disclose them in the notes to the financial statements, being careful not to give misleading implications about the likelihood of their being realized.

Executory Contracts

Executory (unperformed) contracts or agreements, such as *purchase agreements* and *lines of credit*, usually are **not** recorded because a transfer of assets or liabilities has not yet occurred. However, if the anticipated considerations are material, **note disclosure** is required.

Current Liabilities and Contingencies

Concept Review

1. The three essential characteristics of liabilities for purposes of financial reporting are that liabilities:
   a. are probable, _____ sacrifices of economic benefits.
   b. that arise from _____ obligations (to transfer goods or provide services) to other entities.
   c. that result from _____ transactions or events.

2. In most cases, current liabilities are obligations payable within one year or within the firm's _____ , whichever is longer.

3. _____ are obligations to suppliers of merchandise or of services purchased on open account.

4. Trade notes payable differ from accounts payable in that they are formally recognized by a written _____ . Often these are of a somewhat _____ term than open accounts and sometimes bear _____ .

5. A _____ allows a company to borrow cash without having to follow formal loan procedures and paperwork.

6. Interest payable on notes is calculated as: face amount x annual rate x _____ .

7. When interest is "discounted" from the face amount of a note, the effective interest rate is _____ than the stated discount rate.

8. _____ refers to unsecured notes usually sold to other corporations in minimum denominations of $25,000 with maturities ranging from 30 to 270 days.

9. _____ represent expenses already incurred, but for which cash has yet to be paid (accrued expenses), recorded by adjusting entries at the end of the reporting period.

10. Collecting cash from a customer as a refundable deposit or as an advance payment for products or services, creates a _____ .

11. Sales taxes collected from customers represent _____ until remitted.

12. Long-term liabilities that are due on demand – by terms of the contract or violation of contract covenants – must be reported as _____ .

13. Short-term obligations can be reported as noncurrent liabilities if the company (a) *intends* to _____ and (b) demonstrates the _____ .

14. A _____ involves an existing uncertainty as to whether a loss really exists, where the uncertainty will be resolved only when some future event occurs.

15. A liability is accrued if it is both _____ that the confirming event will occur and the amount can be at least _____ .

16. A loss contingency must be disclosed in notes to the financial statements if there is at least a _____ that the loss will occur.

17. The estimated amount of cash rebates or the cost of noncash premiums estimated to be given out represents both _____ and _____ in the reporting period the product is sold.

18. Events occurring after the year-end but before _____ can be used to clarify the nature of financial statement elements at the report date.

19. It must be _____ that an unasserted claim or assessment or an unfiled lawsuit will occur before considering whether and how to report the possible loss.

20. _____ contingencies are not accrued.

Answers:
1. a. future, b. present, c. past 2. operating cycle 3. Accounts payable 4. promissory note, longer, interest 5. line of credit 6. time to maturity 7. higher 8. Commercial paper
9. Accrued liabilities 10. liability to return the deposit or to supply the products or services 11. liabilities 12. current liabilities 13. (a) refinance on a long-term basis and (b) *ability* to do so by a refinancing agreement or by actual financing 14. loss contingency 15. Probable, reasonably estimated 16. reasonable possibility 17. an expense, estimated liability
18. financial statements are issued 19. probable 20. Gain

REVIEW EXERCISES

Exercise 1

On October 1, 2003, Alexander Supplies borrowed $300,000 cash from First Bank under a line of credit arrangement. Alexander issued a 5-month, 8% promissory note. Alexander's fiscal period is the calendar year. Interest was payable at maturity.

Required:

1. Prepare the journal entry for the issuance of the note.

2. Prepare the appropriate adjusting entry for the note on December 31, 2003.

3. Prepare the journal entry for the payment of the note at maturity.

Solution:

Requirement 1

Cash	300,000	
Notes payable		300,000

Requirement 2

Interest expense ($300,000 x 8% x $3/12$)	6,000	
Interest payable..		6,000

Requirement 3

Interest expense ($300,000 x 8% x $2/12$)	4,000	
Interest payable (from adjusting entry)	6,000	
Notes payable (face amount)...	300,000	
Cash (total)		310,000

Exercise 2

Suppose the note in the previous exercise was a "noninterest-bearing note" and 8% is the bank's stated "discount rate."

Required:

1. Prepare the journal entry for the issuance of the note.

2. Prepare the appropriate adjusting entry for the note on December 31, 2000.

3. Prepare the journal entry for the payment of the note at maturity.

Solution:

Requirement 1

Cash (difference)..	290,000	
Discount on notes payable ($300,000 x 8% x $5/_{12}$)	10,000	
Notes payable (face amount)..		300,000

Requirement 2

Interest expense ($300,000 x 8% x $3/_{12}$)[*]	6,000	
Discount on notes payable		6,000

[*] or, ($290,000 x 8.27584% x $3/_{12}$) = $6,000

    The effective interest rate is 8.27584% ($10,000 ÷ $290,000) x $12/_5$.

Requirement 3

Interest expense ($300,000 x 8% x $2/_{12}$)[*]	4,000	
Discount on notes payable		4,000
Notes payable (face amount)...	300,000	
Cash		300,000

[*] or, ($290,000 x 8.27584% x $2/_{12}$) = $4,000

    The effective interest rate is 8.27584% ($10,000 ÷ $290,000) x $12/_5$.

Exercise 3

General Phil's Cereal offers a VCR (Voodoo Code Reader) in exchange for 5 return box tops. Funzy estimates that 40% will be redeemed. The cardboard and plastic VCRs cost the company $.50. 600,000 boxes of cereal were sold in 2003. By the end of the year 90,000 box tops had been redeemed.

Required:

Calculate the **liability** that General Phil's Cereal should report at December 31, 2003.

Solution:

600,000 x 40% = 240,000		Box tops expected to be redeemed
	÷ 5	
	48,000	Total VCRs expected
90,000 ÷ 5 =	18,000	VCRs issued
	30,000	VCRs to be issued
	x $.50	
	$15,000	Liability

MULTIPLE CHOICE

Enter the letter corresponding to the response which **best** completes each of the following statements or questions.

_____ 1. The essential characteristics of a liability do **not** include:
    a.   The existence of a past causal transaction or event.
    b.   Present obligation.
    c.   The existence of a legal obligation.
    d.   A future sacrifice of economic benefits.

_____ 2. Of the following, which usually would **not** be classified as a current liability?
    a.   A nine-month note to be paid with the proceeds from the sale of common stock.
    b.   Bonds payable maturing within the coming year.
    c.   Estimated warranty liability.
    d.   Subscription revenue received in advance.

_____ 3. Which of the following results in an accrued liability?

	Interest on a 6 month bank loan due in two months	Sales taxes collected on recent sales
a.	Yes	Yes
b.	Yes	No
c.	No	No
d.	No	Yes

_____ 4. On November 1, 2003, Epic Distributors borrowed $24 million cash to fund an expansion of its facilities. The loan was made by WW BancCorp under a short-term line of credit. Epic issued a 9-month, 12% promissory note. Interest was payable at maturity. Epic's fiscal period is the calendar year. In Epic's adjusting entry for the note on December 31, 2003, **interest expense** will be:
   a. $0
   b. $240,000
   c. $480,000
   d. $640,000

_____ 5. On October 1, 2003, Parton Industries borrowed $12 million cash to provide working capital. The loan was made by Second Bank under a short-term line of credit. Parton issued an 8-month, "noninterest-bearing note." 8% is the bank's stated "discount rate." Parton's fiscal period is the calendar year. In Parton's 2003 income statement **interest expense** for the note will be:
   a. $0
   b. $240,000
   c. $360,000
   d. $480,000

_____ 6. Commercial paper has become an increasingly popular way for companies to raise funds. Which of the following is **not** true regarding commercial paper?
   a. Commercial paper is often purchased by other companies as a short-term investment.
   b. Commercial paper usually is sold in minimum denominations of $25,000 with maturities of greater than 270 days.
   c. Interest often is discounted at the issuance of the note.
   d. Usually the interest rate is lower than in a bank loan.

_____ 7. On November 1, 2003, Shearer Shoes borrowed $18 million cash and issued a 6-month, "noninterest-bearing note." The loan was made by Third Commercial Bank whose stated "discount rate" is 9%. Shearer's effective interest rate on this loan is:
   a. 8.61%
   b. 9%
   c. 9.42%
   d. 9.5%

_____ 8.   Liabilities payable within one year can be **excluded** from current liabilities only if:
   a.   The business intends to refinance the obligations on a long-term basis.
   b.   The business has the demonstrated ability to refinance the obligations on a long-term basis.
   c.   Both a and b.
   d.   Liabilities payable within one year always must be classified as current liabilities.

_____ 9.   Reunion BBQ has $4,000,000 of notes payable due on March 11, 2004, which Reunion intends to refinance. On January 5, 2004, Reunion signed a line of credit agreement to borrow up to $3,500,000 cash on a two-year renewable basis. On the December 31, 2003, balance sheet, Reunion should classify:
   a. $500,000 of notes payable as short-term and $3,500,000 as long-term obligations.
   b. $500,000 of notes payable as long-term and $3,500,000 as short-term obligations.
   c. $4,000,000 of notes payable as short-term obligations.
   d. $4,000,000 of notes payable as long-term obligations.

_____ 10.   Which of the following statements concerning lines of credit is **untrue**?
   a.   A line of credit is an agreement that permits a company to borrow up to a prearranged limit without having to follow formal loan procedures and paperwork.
   b.   A *noncommitted* line of credit is a formal agreement that usually requires the firm to pay a commitment fee to the bank.
   c.   Banks sometimes require the company to maintain a compensating balance on deposit with the bank (say 5%) as part of the line of credit agreement.
   d.   Most short-term bank loans are arranged under an existing line of credit.

_____ 11.   In its 2003 financial statements, an enterprise should accrue a liability for a loss contingency involving a possible cash payment if certain conditions exist. Each of the following is a condition for accrual except:
   a.   The payment is probable.
   b.   The cause of the loss contingency occurred prior to the end of 2003.
   c.   The amount of payment can be estimated before the 2003 financial statements are issued.
   d.   The obligation is a legally enforceable claim.

_____ 12.   Which of the following loss contingencies generally do **not** require accrual?
   a.   Manufacturers' product guarantees.
   b.   Claims by government agencies with probable negative outcomes.
   c.   Obligations due to cash rebate offers.
   d.   Retailers' extended warranties.

_____ 13.   Warren Advertising becomes aware of a lawsuit after the end of the fiscal year, but prior to the issuance of financial statements. A loss should be accrued and a liability should be reported if the amount can be reasonably estimated and:
   a.   The cause for action occurred prior to the end of the fiscal year.
   b.   The damages would be payable within a year.
   c.   Both a. and b.
   d.   The contingency should not be accrued.

_____ 14. A loss contingency should be accrued when the amount of loss is known and the occurrence of the loss is:

	Remote	**Reasonably possible**
a.	No	No
b.	Yes	Yes
c.	Yes	No
d.	No	Yes

_____ 15. During 2003 Green Thumb Company introduced a new line of garden shears that carry a two-year warranty against defects. Experience indicates that warranty costs should be 2% of net sales in the year of sale and 3% in the year after sale. Net sales and actual warranty expenditures were as follows:

	Net sales	**Actual warranty expenditures**
2003	$ 45,000	$1,000
2004	120,000	3,500

At December 31, 2004, Green Thumb should report as a warranty **liability** of:
   a. $900
   b. $1,250
   c. $3,750
   d. $4,500

_____ 16. There is a possibility of a safety hazard for a manufactured product. As yet, no claim has been made for damages, though there is a reasonable possibility that a claim will be made. If a claim is made, it is probable that damages will be paid and the amount of the loss can be reasonably estimated. This possible loss must be:

	Accrued	**Disclosed**
a.	Yes	Yes
b.	Yes	No
c.	No	Yes
d.	No	No

_____ 17. Gain contingencies usually are recognized in the income statement when:
   a. The gain is realized.
   b. The gain is probable and the amount is known.
   c. The gain is probable and the amount can be reasonably estimated.
   d. The gain is reasonably possible and the amount can be reasonably estimated.

Answers:

1.	c	6.	b	11.	d	16.	d
2.	a	7.	c	12.	d	17.	a
3.	b	8.	c	13.	c		
4.	c	9.	a	14.	a		
5.	b	10.	b	15.	c		

14

Bonds and Long-Term Notes

LEARNING OBJECTIVES

After studying this chapter, you should be able to:

1. Identify the underlying characteristics of debt instruments and describe the basic approach to accounting for debt.
2. Account for bonds issued at par, at a discount, or at a premium, recording interest at the effective rate or by the straight-line method.
3. Characterize the accounting treatment of notes, including installment notes, issued for cash or for noncash consideration.
4. Describe the disclosures appropriate to long-term debt in its various forms.
5. Record the early extinguishment of debt and its conversion into equity securities.

CHAPTER HIGHLIGHTS

The Nature of Long-Term Debt

A liability requires the future payment of cash in specified amounts, at specified dates. As time passes, interest accrues on debt at the effective interest rate times the amount of the debt outstanding during the period. This same principle applies regardless of the specific form of the liability.

Liabilities signify various creditors' interest in a company's assets. Debt requires the future payment of cash in specified (or estimated) amounts, at specified (or projected) dates. A liability is reported at the present value of its related cash flows (interest and/or principal payments), discounted at the effective rate of interest at issuance.

PART A: BONDS

Bond Indenture

A bond indenture describes the specific promises made to bondholders. Debenture bonds are secured only by the "full faith and credit" of the issuing corporation as opposed to mortgage bonds

Bonds and Long-Term Notes

which are backed by liens on specified real estate owned by the issuer. Most corporate bonds are callable, or redeemable. The call feature permits the issuing company to buy back, or "call," outstanding bonds from bondholders before their scheduled maturity date.

Pricing Bonds

All bonds are *priced to yield the market rate*. This means a bond's price is calculated as the *present value* of all the cash flows required, where the discount rate is the market rate at date of issue. The market rate is influenced by the risk, as perceived by investors, of the company not paying interest or principal as scheduled. Other things being equal, the lower the perceived riskiness of the corporation issuing bonds, the higher the price those bonds will command.

Illustration

On January 1, 2003, Woods Golf Gear issued $100,000 of 8% bonds, dated January 1. Interest of $4,000 is payable semiannually on June 30 and December 31. The bonds mature in four years. The market rate for bonds of similar risk and maturity is 10% (5% semiannually). The entire bond issue was purchased by Ruth-Aaron Industries.

Calculation of the price of the bonds:

			Present Values
Interest	$4,000 x 6.46321 * =		$25,853
Principal	$100,000 x 0.67684 ** =		67,684
Present value (price) of the bonds			$93,537

* Present value of an ordinary annuity of $1: n=8, i=5% (Table 6A-4)

** Present value of $1: n=8, i=5% (Table 6A-2)

Journal entry at issuance:

Woods Golf Gear (Issuer)		
Cash (price calculated above)	93,537	
Discount on bonds payable (difference)	6,463	
Bonds payable (face amount)...		100,000
Ruth-Aaron Industries (Investor)		
Investment in bonds (face amount)	100,000	
Discount on bond investment (difference)..............................		6,463
Cash (price calculated above)		93,537

All bonds sell at their price plus any interest that has accrued since the last interest date. Because the Woods Golf Gear bonds were not issued between interest dates, there was no accrued interest.

Interest on Bonds

Interest accrues at the *effective market rate of interest multiplied by the outstanding balance* (during the interest period). A company is permitted to allocate a discount or a premium equally to each period over the term to maturity (straight-line method) as long as doing so produces results that are not materially different from the effective interest method.

Interest at June 30, 2003:

Woods Golf Gear (Issuer)		
Interest expense (5% x $93,537)...	4,677	
Discount on bonds payable (difference).......................................		677
Cash (4% x $100,000)..		4,000
Ruth-Aaron Industries(Investor)		
Cash (4% x $100,000)...	4,000	
Discount on bond investment (difference)......................................	677	
Interest revenue (5% x $93,537)..		4,677

Bonds and Long-Term Notes

Amortization Schedule

Interest in this and every period is the effective market rate of interest multiplied by the outstanding balance. Because the outstanding balance changes each period, the dollar amount of interest also will change each period. To keep up with the changing amounts, it's convenient to prepare an amortization schedule. For Woods and Ruth-Aaron, the amortization schedule to determine the effective interest is:

Date	Cash interest *stated rate x face amount* **4%**	Effective interest *effective rate x balance* **5%**	Change in Balance	Outstanding Balance
01/01/2003				93,537
06/30/2003	4,000	.05 (93,537) = 4,677	677	94,214
12/31/2003	4,000	.05 (94,214) = 4,711	711	94,925
06/30/2004	4,000	.05 (94,925) = 4,746	746	95,671
12/31/2004	4,000	.05 (95,671) = 4,784	784	96,455
06/30/2005	4,000	.05 (96,455) = 4,823	823	97,278
12/31/2005	4,000	.05 (97,278) = 4,864	864	98,142
06/30/2006	4,000	.05 (98,142) = 4,907	907	99,049
12/31/2006	4,000	.05 (99,049) = 4,951*	951	100,000
	32,000	**38,463**	**6,463**	

* rounded

Straight-line Method

A company is permitted to allocate a discount or a premium equally to each period over the term to maturity as long as doing so produces results that are not materially different from the effective interest method. By the straight-line method, the entries to record interest will be the same each period until maturity:

Interest at June 30, 2003:

Woods Golf Gear (Issuer)

Interest expense (to balance)...	4,808	
Discount on bonds payable ($6,463 ÷ 8 periods)........................		808
Cash (stated rate x face amount)		4,000

Ruth-Aaron Industries(Investor)

Cash (stated rate x face amount)......................................	4,000	
Discount on bond investment ($6,463 ÷ 8 periods)........................	808	
Interest revenue (to balance)		4,808

Bond Issue Costs

Costs incurred in connection with the issuance of bonds, such as legal costs, printing costs, and underwriting fees, are recorded separately and are amortized over the term of the related bonds. These costs generally are debited to a "bond issue costs" account and amortized on a straight-line basis.

Zero-Coupon Bonds

A zero-coupon bond pays no interest but, rather, offers a return in the form of a "deep discount" at issuance from the face amount.

PART B: LONG-TERM NOTES

In concept, notes are accounted for in precisely the same way as bonds. The stated interest rate on a note is likely to be the same as the market rate because the rate usually is negotiated at the time of the loan. As a result, discounts and premiums are less likely than on bonds.

Unrealistic Interest Rate

When a note is issued in exchange for a noncash asset (or service), the stated interest rate usually is appropriate and in keeping with the market rate for the type of transaction. However, if a note is issued on which the stated interest rate is unrealistic, the effective market rate is used both to determine the amount recorded in the transaction and to record periodic interest thereafter. Stated differently, if the asset (or service) received has a fair value different from the face amount of the note, both the asset and note are recorded at the fair value of whichever is easier to determine. If fair value of neither is known, the transaction is recorded at the present value of the note, discounted at the market rate of interest. The accounting treatment is the same whether the amount is determined directly from the market value of the asset (and thus the note, also) or indirectly as the present value of the note (and thus the value of the asset).

Illustration

Winburn Corporation purchased a custom-made machine and signed a 3-year, $40,000, 5% note. Interest of $2,000 is payable annually. The "market" rate of interest is 12%.

Calculation of the present value of the note:

				Present Values
Interest	$2,000 x	2.40183 * =		$ 4,804
Principal	$40,000 x	0.71178 ** =		28,471
Present value (price) of the note				$33,275

   *   Present value of an ordinary annuity of $1: n=3, i=12% (Table 6A-4)
 ** Present value of $1: n=3, i=12% (Table 6A-2)

To record the purchase of the machine and issuance of the note:

Machine	33,275	
Discount on note	6,725	
Note payable		40,000

Both parties to the transaction should record periodic interest (interest *expense* to the *borrower*, interest *revenue* to the *lender*) at the effective rate, rather than the stated rate.

To keep up with the changing amounts, it's convenient to prepare an **amortization schedule**:

Date	Cash interest *stated rate x face amount* **5%**	Effective interest *effective rate x balance* **12%**		Change in **Balance**	Outstanding **Balance**
					33,275
2003	2,000	.12(33,275) =	3,993	1,993	35,268
2004	2,000	.12(35,268) =	4,232	2,232	37,500
2005	2,000	.12(37,500) =	4,500	2,500	40,000
	6,000		12,725	6,725	

To record the periodic interest on the note:

	2003	2004	2004
Interest expense	3,993	4,232	4,500
Discount on note	1,993	2,232	2,500
Cash	2,000	2,000	2,000

To the record the payment of the note:

Note payable	40,000	
Cash...		40,000

Installment Notes

Some notes are paid in installments, rather than by a single amount at maturity. The installment payments are equal amounts each period. Each payment includes both an amount that represents interest and an amount that represents a reduction of principal. The periodic reduction of principal is sufficient that, at maturity, the note is completely paid.

© *The McGraw-Hill Companies, Inc., 2001*

The installment amount can be calculated by dividing the amount of the loan by the appropriate discount factor for the present value of an annuity. For example, if a $40,000, 10% loan is to be repaid with three year-end installment payments, each payment would be:

$$\underset{\substack{\text{amount} \\ \text{of loan}}}{\$40,000} \;\div\; 2.48685^* \;=\; \underset{\substack{\text{installment} \\ \text{payment}}}{\$16,085}$$

- Present value of an ordinary annuity of $1: n=3, i=10% (Table 6A-4)

Financial Statement Disclosures

To provide adequate disclosure, additional information is provided in footnotes to the financial statements. Supplemental disclosure is required of the *fair value* of bonds, notes, and other financial instruments. Disclosure also should include, for all long-term borrowings, the aggregate amounts maturing and sinking fund requirements (if any) for each of the next five years.

PART C: DEBT RETIRED EARLY, CONVERTIBLE INTO STOCK, OR PROVIDING AN OPTION TO BUY STOCK

Early Extinguishment of Debt

A gain or a loss may result when debt is retired before its scheduled maturity. Any gain or loss on early extinguishment of debt should be recorded for the difference between the price paid to retire the debt and the carrying amount of the debt. The gain or loss should be reported on the income statement as an *extraordinary item*.

Convertible Debt

Convertible bonds are bonds that are convertible into a specified number of shares of common stock. Although the conversion privilege has market value, it is not separately recorded. Thus, they are accounted for as straight debt; that is, in exactly the same manner as if the bonds were nonconvertible.

If and when the bondholder exercises the option to convert the bonds into stock, the bonds are removed from the accounting records and the new shares issued are recorded at the same amount (that is, at the book value of the bonds). For example, if the bonds in the previous illustration had been convertible, we would have accounted for them in precisely the same way as we did when we assumed they were not convertible. If half of the $100,000 bonds were converted into 10,000 shares of $1 par common stock at a time when the remaining unamortized discount was $1,858, the entry would be:

Convertible bonds payable (¹/₂ the account balance)............................	50,000	
Discount on bonds payable (¹/₂ the account balance)...................		929
Common stock (10,000 shares x $1 par)......................................		10,000
Paid-in capital– excess of par (to balance)................................		39,071

Debt With Detachable Warrants

Bonds with detachable warrants also permit the investor to acquire a specified number of shares of common stock, usually at a specified option price. Because stock warrants have value and are traded separately in the market, two different securities actually are being sold for a single price.

So, the value of the equity feature is recorded separately for bonds issued with detachable warrants. At issuance, the price should be allocated between the two different securities: the bonds (debt) and the warrants (equity). If the separate market value of only one of the two securities is determinable, that market value determines the allocation.

APPENDIX 14-A: TROUBLED DEBT RESTRUCTURING

The way a troubled debt restructuring is recorded depends on whether (1) the debt is *settled* at the time of the restructuring, or (2) the debt is *continued*, but with *modified terms* where the total cash to be paid (a) *is less than* the carrying amount of the debt or (b) *exceeds* the carrying amount of the debt.

Debt Settled

When debt is settled at the time of the restructuring, the debtor records a *gain* equal to the difference between the carrying amount of the debt and the fair value of whatever is paid in accordance with the agreement. For instance, a bank holding a $10 million note might agree to accept land valued at $7 million as final settlement of the debt. If so, the debtor has a $3 million extraordinary gain equal to the difference between the carrying amount of the debt and the fair value of the land transferred. The debtor may need to adjust the carrying amount of an asset to its fair value before recording its exchange for the note.

Debt Continued With Modified Terms – Total Cash to be Paid is Less Than the Debt

A bank might allow a debt to continue, but modify the terms of the debt agreement to make it easier for the debtor to comply. If the new agreement calls for less cash than the amount now owed, interest is presumed to have been eliminated. Therefore, after the debt restructuring no interest expense is recorded. All subsequent cash payments are considered to be payment of the debt itself.

Illustration

Floyd Company owes First Bank $10 million, under a 10% note with 2 years remaining to maturity. Due to Floyd's financial difficulties, the previous year's interest ($1 million) was not paid. First Bank agrees to accept 2 payments of $4 million each beginning one year from now.

Analysis:

Carrying amount:	$10 million + $1 million =	$11 million
Future payments:	$4 million x 2 =	8 million
Gain		$ 3 million

	($ in millions)	
Accrued interest payable (10% x $10 million).................................	1	
Note payable ($10 million – $8 million)...	2	
Gain (extraordinary) on debt restructuring		3

No interest should be recorded thereafter. Each of the two cash payments result in reductions of principal:

	($ in millions)	
Note payable	4	
Cash..		4
Note payable	4	
Cash..		4

Debt Continued With Modified Terms – Total Cash to be Paid is More Than the Debt

If the new agreement calls for more cash than the amount now owed, interest is presumed to remain. Therefore, after the debt restructuring interest expense is recorded, but at a new rate. The accounting objective now is to determine what the new effective rate is and record interest for the remaining term of the loan at that new, lower rate.

SELF-STUDY QUESTIONS AND EXERCISES

Concept Review

1. Liabilities ordinarily should be valued at the _____ of future cash flows.

2. Periodic interest is calculated as the _____ interest rate times the amount of the debt outstanding during the period.

3. All of the specific promises made to bondholders are described in a _____ . This formal agreement will specify the bond issue's face amount, the stated interest rate, the method of paying interest (whether the bonds are registered bonds or coupon bonds), whether the bonds are backed by a lien on specified assets, and whether they are subordinated to other debt.

4. In order for a company to sell its bonds that pay a 10% stated interest in an 11% market, the bonds would have to be priced at a _____ from face amount. This would be the amount that causes the bond issue to be priced to yield ____%.

5. An inverse relationship exists between the prevailing market rate of interest and the _____ of bonds.

6. A _____ related to a bond issue should be classified as a contra-liability and amortized over the term to maturity.

7. The _____ method is required in amortizing bond discounts or premiums, unless the use of the _____ method would not produce materially different results.

8. The _____ method results in a *constant dollar amount* of interest each period. By the _____ method, the dollar amounts of interest vary over the term to maturity because the *percentage rate* of interest remains constant, but is applied to a changing debt balance.

9. When bonds are issued at a _____ the debt *declines* each period because the effective interest each period is *less than* the cash interest paid.

10. The carrying value of a bond increases over the term to maturity if the bond is sold at a _____ .

11. When bonds are issued between interest dates, it's necessary to calculate _____ from when the bonds are dated to the date of issuance.

12. A note issued solely for cash is presumed to have a present value equal to the _____ .

13. When notes are paid in installments, rather than a single amount at maturity, installment payments typically are equal amounts each period. Each payment will include both an amount representing _____ and an amount representing a reduction of _____ .

14. The entire issue price of convertible bonds is recorded as _____ , precisely the same way, in fact, as for nonconvertible bonds.

15. The issue price of bonds with _____ is allocated between the two different securities on the basis of their market values.

16. Upon the early extinguishment of debt, any gain or loss is to be reported as an extraordinary item if it is both _____ and infrequent.

17. Regardless of the method used to retire debt prior to its scheduled maturity date, the gain or loss on the transaction is simply the difference between the _____ of the debt at that time and the cash paid to retire it.

18. For all long-term borrowings, disclosure should include (a) the fair values, (b) the aggregate amounts maturing, and (c) sinking fund requirements (if any) for each of the next _____ years.

19. A _____ involves some concessions on the part of the creditor (lender).

20. In a troubled debt restructuring, when the total future cash payments are less than the carrying amount of the debt, the difference is recorded as a _____ to the debtor at the date of restructure. No interest is recorded thereafter. All subsequent cash payments produce reductions of _____ .

21. A continuation of debt under a troubled debt restructuring involving modified terms requires a recalculation of the _____ if the total future cash payments exceed the carrying amount of the debt.

Answers:
1. present value **2.** effective **3.** bond indenture **4.** discount, 11 **5.** market price **6.** discount
7. effective interest; straight-line **8.** straight-line, effective interest **9.** premium
10. discount **11.** accrued interest **12.** cash proceeds **13.** interest, principal **14.** debt **15.** detachable warrants **16.** unusual **17.** carrying amount **18.** five **19.** troubled debt restructuring **20.** gain, principal **21.** effective rate of interest

REVIEW EXERCISES

Exercise 1

Kelly Industries issued 11% bonds, dated January 1, with a face value of $100 million on January 1, 2003. The bonds mature in 2012 (10 years). Interest is paid semiannually on June 30 and December 31. For bonds of similar risk and maturity the market yield is 12%.

Required:

a. Determine the price of the bonds at January 1, 2003. **Show calculations.**

b. Prepare the journal entry to record their issuance by Kelly Industries on January 1, 2003.

c. Prepare the journal entry to record interest on June 30, 2003 (at the effective rate). [You are not required to prepare an amortization schedule.] **Show calculations.**

d. Prepare the journal entry to record interest on December 31, 2003 (at the effective rate). [You are not required to prepare an amortization schedule.] **Show calculations.**

Solution:

a. Price of the bonds at January 1, 2003

Interest	$5,500,000	x	11.46992 *(from Table 6A-2)* =	$63,084,560
	(5.5% x $100,000,000)		*n=20, i=6%*	
Principal	$100,000,000	x	0.31180 *(from Table 6A-4)* =	31,180,000
			n=20, i=6%	
Present value (price) of the bonds				$94,264,560

b. Journal entry to record their issuance on January 1, 2003

Cash (price determined above)	94,264,560	
Discount on bonds (difference)...	5,735,440	
Bonds payable (face value)..		100,000,000

c. Journal entry to record interest on June 30, 2003

Interest expense (6% x $94,264,560)..	5,655,874	
Discount on bonds payable (difference)		155,874
Cash (5.5% x $100,000,000)		5,500,000

d. Journal entry to record interest on December 31, 2003

Interest expense (6% x [$94,264,560 + 155,874])....................	5,665,226	
Discount on bonds payable (difference)		165,226
Cash (5.5% x $100,000,000)		5,500,000

Exercise 2

On July 1, 2003, Richardson Foods issued $100 million of its 8%, bonds for $92 million. The bonds were priced to yield 10%. The bonds are dated July 1, 2003. Interest is payable semiannually on December 31 and June 30. Richardson records interest at the effective rate.

Required:

a. Prepare the journal entry to record interest on December 31, 2003 (the **first** interest payment). **Show calculations.**

b. Prepare the journal entry to record interest on June 30, 2004 (the **second** interest payment). **Show calculations.**

Bonds and Long-Term Notes

> *Solution:*
>
> a. Interest expense (5% x $92 million) 4,600,000
>   Discount on bonds payable (difference)   600,000
>   Cash (4% x $100 million)..   4,000,000
>
> b. Interest expense (5% x [$92 million + .6 million])................. 4,630,000
>   Discount on bonds payable (difference)   630,000
>   Cash (4% x $100 million)..   4,000,000

Exercise 3

Pilot Products borrowed $800,000 from First Bank on January 1, 2002, and signed a three-year note with a stated interest rate of 12%. Interest is payable in full at maturity on December 31, 2004.

Required:

Determine the amount Pilot Products should report as a liability for accrued interest at December 31, 2003. **Show calculations.**

> *Solution:*
>
> | | |
> |---|---|
> | $800,000 | Face amount |
> | x 12% | Interest rate |
> | $ 96,000 | First year interest |
> | 800,000 | Face amount |
> | $896,000 | Carrying amount during second year |
> | x 12% | Interest rate |
> | $107,520 | Second year interest |
> | 96,000 | First year interest |
> | $203,520 | Accrued interest at December 31, 2003 |

MULTIPLE CHOICE

Enter the letter corresponding to the response that **best** completes each of the following statements or questions.

____ 1. On September 1, 2003, Expert Materials, issued at 98 plus accrued interest, $800,000 of its 10% bonds. The bonds are dated June 1, 2003, and mature on May 30, 2013. Interest is payable semiannually on June 1 and December 1. At the time of issuance, Expert would receive cash of:
   a. $784,000
   b. $803,600
   c. $804,000
   d. $820,000

____ 2. On September 1, 2003, Contemporary Products, issued $16 million of its 10% bonds at face value. The bonds are dated June 1, 2003, and mature on May 30, 2013. Interest is payable semiannually on June 1 and December 1. At the time of issuance, Contemporary Products would receive cash proceeds that would include accrued interest of:
   a.   Zero.
   b. $200,000 .
   c. $400,000.
   d. $1.6 million.

____ 3. The price of a corporate bond is the present value of its face amount at the market or effective rate of interest:
   a.   Plus the present value of all future interest payments at the market or effective rate of interest.
   b.   Plus the present value of all future interest payments at the stated rate of interest.
   c.   Reduced by the present value of all future interest payments at the market or effective rate of interest.
   d.   Reduced by the present value of all future interest payments at the stated rate of interest.

____ 4. When a bond issue sells for less than its face value, the market rate of interest is:
   a.   Dependent on the stated rate of interest.
   b.   Equal to the stated rate of interest.
   c.   Higher than the stated rate of interest.
   d.   Less than the stated rate of interest.

Bonds and Long-Term Notes

___ 5. On June 30, 2003, Mabry Corporation issued $5 million of its 8% bonds for $4.6 million. The bonds were priced to yield 10%. The bonds are dated June 30, 2003, and mature on June 30, 2013. Interest is payable semiannually on December 31 and July 1. If the effective interest method is used, by how much should the bond discount be reduced for the 6 months ended December 31, 2003?
   a. $16,000
   b. $20,000
   c. $23,000
   d. $30,000

___ 6. A discount on bonds should be reported on the balance sheet:
   a. At the present value of the future addition to bond interest expense due to the discount.
   b. As a reduction in bond issue costs.
   c. As a reduction of the face amount of the bond.
   d. As a deferred credit.

___ 7. If bonds are issued between interest dates the entry to record the issuance of the bonds will:
   a. Include a credit to accrued interest payable.
   b. Include a debit to interest expense.
   c. Include a debit to cash that has been reduced by accrued interest from the last interest date.
   d. Be unaffected by the timing of sale.

___ 8. On January 1, 2003, Blair Company sold $800,000 of 10% ten-year bonds. Interest is payable semiannually on June 30 and December 31. The bonds were sold for $708,000, priced to yield 12%. Blair records interest at the effective rate. Blair should report bond interest expense for the six months ended June 30, 2003 in the amount of:
   a. $35,400
   b. $40,000
   c. $42,480
   d. $48,000

___ 9. In a bond amortization table for bonds issued at a discount:
   a. The effective interest expense is less with each successive interest payment.
   b. The total effective interest over the term to maturity is equal to the amount of the discount plus the total cash interest paid.
   c. The outstanding balance (carrying amount) of the bonds declines eventually to face value.
   d. The reduction in the discount is less with each successive interest payment.

____ 10. Bonds will sell at:
    a. Their face value if the stated rate is equal to the nominal rate.
    b. Their face value unless the stated rate is less than the market rate.
    c. A discount if the stated rate exceeds the market rate.
    d. A premium if the stated rate exceeds the market rate.

____ 11. When bonds are issued at a discount and interest expense is recorded at the effective interest rate, interest expense in the earlier years of the term to maturity will be:
    a. Less than the cash interest payments made.
    b. Less than if the straight-line method were used.
    c. Greater that if the straight-line method were used.
    d. The same as if the straight-line method were used.

____ 12. AMC Corporation issued bonds at a discount. The long-term liability reported on AMC's balance sheet will:
    a. Increase each year during the term to maturity.
    b. Decrease each year during the term to maturity.
    c. Remain the same each year during the term to maturity.
    d. Increase or decrease each year depending upon the market rate of interest.

____ 13. When a firm records bond interest at the effective rate for bonds issued at a discount, its net income in the bond's first year will be:
    a. Less than if the straight-line method were used.
    b. Higher than if the straight-line method were used.
    c. The same as if the straight-line method were used.
    d. None of the above.

____ 14. BVA Corporation exchanged a $96,000, noninterest-bearing, 3-year note for land with a fair value of $60,000. The $36,000 difference represents:
    a. A loss on the purchase of land.
    b. A premium on notes payable.
    c. Interest expense to be recorded over three years.
    d. None of the above.

____ 15. When a note is issued in exchange for a machine, and interest on the note is not stated:
   a. The machine should be depreciated over the term to maturity of the note.
   b. The note should be recorded at its present value, discounted at an appropriate market rate of interest, if fair values of the note and machine are unavailable.
   c. The note and machine are recorded at the face amount of the note or the fair value of the machine, whichever is more clearly determinable.
   d. The note is recorded at its face amount unless the fair market value of the machine is readily available.

____ 16. Brown Corporation exercised its call option to retire long-term notes. The excess of the cash paid over the carrying amount of the notes should be reported as a(an):
   a. Gain from discontinued operations.
   b. Gain from continuing operations.
   c. Loss from discontinued operations.
   d. Loss from continuing operations.

____ 17. National Storage issued $90 million of its 10% bonds on April 1, 2003, at 99 plus accrued interest. The bonds are dated January 1, 2003, and mature on December 31, 2024. Interest is payable semiannually on June 30 and December 31. What amount did National receive from the bond issuance?
   a. $86.85 million
   b. $89.10 million
   c. $90.00 million
   d. $91.35 million

____ 18. On March 1, 2003, Big Brands Corporation issued $600,000 of 10% bonds at 105. Each $1,000 bond was sold with 50 detachable stock warrants, each permitting the investor to purchase one share of common stock for $35. On that date, the market value of the common stock was $30 per share and the market value of each warrant was $4. Big Brands should record what amount of the proceeds from the bond issue as an increase in liabilities?
   a. $510,000
   b. $600,000
   c. $630,000
   d. $0

____ 19. On June 30, 2003, Kerr Industries had outstanding $40 million of 8%, convertible bonds that mature on June 30, 2004. Interest is payable each year on June 30 and December 31. The bonds are convertible into 2 million shares of $10 par common stock. At June 30, 2003, the unamortized balance in the discount on bonds payable account was $2 million. On June 30, 2003, half the bonds were converted when Kerr's common stock had a market price of $25 per share. When recording the conversion, Kerr should credit paid-in capital – excess of par:
   a. $8 million
   b. $9 million
   c. $11 million
   d. $12 million

____ 20. During 2003 Belair Company was encountering financial difficulties and seemed likely to default on a $600,000, 10%, four-year note dated January 1, 2001, payable to Second Bank. Interest was last paid on December 31, 2002. On December 31, 2003, Second Bank accepted $500,000 in settlement of the note. Ignoring income taxes, what amount should Belair report as a gain from the debt restructuring in its 2003 income statement?
   a. $40,000
   b. $100,000
   c. $160,000
   d. $0

Answers:

1.	c.	6.	c.	11.	b.	16.	d.
2.	c.	7.	a.	12.	a.	17.	d.
3.	a.	8.	c.	13.	b.	18.	a.
4.	c.	9.	b.	14.	c.	19.	b.
5.	d.	10.	d.	15.	b.	20.	c.

Chapter

15

Leases

LEARNING OBJECTIVES

After studying this chapter, you should be able to:

1. Identify and describe the operational, financial, and tax objectives that motivate leasing.
2. Explain why some leases constitute rental agreements and some represent purchases/sales accompanied by debt financing.
3. Explain the basis for each of the criteria and conditions used to classify leases.
4. Record all transactions associated with operating leases by both the lessor and lessee.
5. Describe and demonstrate how both the lessee and lessor account for a nonoperating lease.
6. Describe and demonstrate how the lessor accounts for a sales-type lease.
7. Explain how lease accounting is affected by the residual value of a leased asset.
8. Describe the way a bargain purchase option affects lease accounting.
9. Explain the impact on lease accounting of executory costs, the discount rate, initial direct costs, and contingent rentals.
10. Explain sale-leaseback agreements and other special leasing arrangements and their accounting treatment.

CHAPTER HIGHLIGHTS

PART A: ACCOUNTING BY THE LESSOR AND LESSEE

For accounting purposes, we classify leases as follows:

LESSEE	**LESSOR**
1. Operating lease	1. Operating lease
2. Capital lease	2. a. Direct financing lease
	b. Sales-type lease

Advantages of Leasing

Companies use leasing for a variety of business reasons. These include using leases as a means of "off-balance-sheet financing" as well as to achieve various operational and tax objectives.

Lease Classification

Consistent with the concept of **substance over form** we account for a lease as either a rental agreement or a purchase/sale accompanied by debt financing. The objective is to "see through" the legal form of the agreement to determine its economic substance and account for it that way.

Lessee

A lessee classifies a lease transaction as a **capital lease** if it is noncancelable and if one or more of four classification criteria are met. Otherwise, it is an operating lease. The criteria are:
1. The agreement specifies that ownership of the asset transfers to the lessee.
2. The agreement contains a bargain purchase option.
3. The noncancelable lease term is equal to *75% or more* of the expected economic life of the asset.
4. The present value of the minimum lease payments is equal to or greater than *90% of the fair value* of the asset.

Lessor

A lessor records a lease as either a direct financing lease or a sales-type lease if one of the four classification criteria is met as well as two additional conditions relating to revenue realization:
1. The collectibility of the lease payments must be reasonably predictable.
2. If any costs to the lessor have yet to be incurred, they are reasonably predictable. (i.e., performance by the lessor is substantially complete.)

Operating Lease

In an operating lease, the lessor does not record a "sale"; the lessee does not record a "purchase." Rather, both parties to the transaction simply record the periodic rental payments as rent: rent revenue by the lessor, rent expense by the lessee. The assumption is that the fundamental rights and responsibilities of ownership are not transferred but retained by the lessor. The lessee is only using the asset temporarily.

Most advance payments are considered prepayments of rent that are deferred and allocated to rent over the lease term. An exception is a refundable security deposit, which is recorded as a long-term *receivable* (by the lessee) and *liability* (by the lessor) unless it is not expected to be returned. Another exception is the prepayment of the last period's rent, which is recorded as prepaid rent and allocated to rent expense/rent revenue during the last period of the lease term.

The cost of a **leasehold improvement** is depreciated (or amortized) over its useful life to the lessee.

Illustration

On January 1, 2003, Cardinal Brands, Inc. leased a computer from Ace Business Equipment. The lease agreement specifies eight quarterly payments of $4,000 beginning March 1, 2003. The useful life of the computer is estimated to be four years. The agreement also specified an advance payment of $8,000 at the inception of the lease. With the permission of Ace, Cardinal Brands purchased and permanently installed additional random access memory to the computer at a cost of $2,000.

January 1, 2003		
Prepaid rent (advance payment)	8,000	
Cash		8,000
Leasehold improvement	2,000	
Cash		2,000
March 1, 2003		
Rent expense (quarterly rent payment)	4,000	
Cash		4,000
Rent expense (advance payment allocation)	1,000	
Prepaid rent ($8,000 ÷ 8)		1,000
Depreciation expense (advance payment allocation)	250	
Accumulated depreciation ($2,000 ÷ 8)		250

Capital Lease – Lessee

A nonoperating lease is recorded by the lessee as a capital lease. In a capital lease the lessee records both an asset and a liability as if an asset were being purchased and paid for with periodic installment payments. Both a leased asset and a lease liability are recorded at the present value of the minimum lease payments.

The discount rate used in the present value computation is the lower of (a) the lessee's incremental borrowing rate and (b) the implicit rate used by the lessor (if known by the lessee) in determining the amount of the periodic payments.

Each lease payment after the inception of the lease includes (a) interest on the lease obligation and (b) a partial reduction of the obligation. As with any other liability, interest expense is recorded at the effective interest rate.

Because the lessee is presumed to have purchased the asset, the lessee normally depreciates the leased asset over the lease term. However, if ownership transfers or a bargain purchase option is present (ownership is expected to transfer) the lessee normally depreciates the leased asset over the asset's useful life. Either way, it's the useful life to the lessee.

Direct Financing Lease – Lessor

A nonoperating lease is recorded by the lessor as a direct financing lease or sales-type lease, depending on whether the lease provides the lessor a dealer's profit (sales-type lease).

In a direct financing lease, the lessor should debit a receivable for the total payments to be made. The difference between the total of the lease payments and the present value of the lease payments to be received over the term of the lease represents unearned interest revenue. The asset's carrying value is removed from the books. The present value of the lease payments and the carrying value of the asset are the same; otherwise, the lease is a sales-type lease. Interest accrues to the lessor at the effective interest rate in a direct financing lease as interest revenue from financing the "purchase" of the asset by the lessee.

Traditionally, the lessee uses the **net method** to record leases, and the lessor uses the **gross method.** Unearned interest revenue is a valuation (contra) account that indirectly reduces the lessor's net receivable.

Illustration

Lessor Company leased equipment to Lessee Company on January 1, 2003. Terms of the lease agreement were as follows:

Lease term: 6 years; 6 annual rent payments, payable at the beginning of each year.
Equipment's fair value: $143,724.
No residual value.
Lessor's required rate of return: 10%
Lessee's incremental borrowing rate: 10%

Lessor Company would compute the **lease payments** as $30,000:

$$\underset{\substack{\text{lessor's}\\\text{cost}}}{\$143,724} \div 4.79079^{**} = \underset{\substack{\text{lease}\\\text{payments}}}{\$30,000}$$

** Present value of an annuity due of $1: n=6, i=10%

Lessee Company would compute the **cost** of the equipment as $143,724:

$$\underset{\substack{\text{lease}\\\text{payments}}}{\$30,000} \times 4.79079^{**} = \underset{\substack{\text{present}\\\text{value}}}{\$143,724}$$

** Present value of an annuity due of $1: n=6, i=10%

The journal entries at the **inception of the lease** are:

Lessor Company			Lessee Company		
Lease receivable	180,000		Leased asset	143,724	
Unearned interest		36,276	Lease liability		143,724
Asset		143,724			
Cash	30,000		Lease liability	30,000	
Lease receivable		30,000	Cash		30,000

Note: The first lease payment includes no interest because no time has passed.

The journal entries for the **second lease payment** are:

Lessor Company			Lessee Company		
Cash	30,000		Lease liability (difference)	18,628	
Lease receivable		30,000	Interest expense	11,372*	
			Cash		30,000
Unearned interest	11,372*				
Interest revenue		11,372*	* 10% x ($143,724 - 30,000)		
			Depreciation expense	23,954	
			($143,724 ÷ 6)		
			Leased property		23,954

Each period the interest is 10% of the outstanding balance. An **amortization schedule** reflecting effective interest can help track the changing amounts:

Payment	Cash	Effective interest effective rate x balance **10%**	Change in Balance	Outstanding Balance
				143,724
1	30,000	0	30,000	113,724
2	30,000	.10 (113,724) = 11,372	18,628	95,096
3	30,000	.10 (95,096) = 9,51020,490	74,606	
4	30,000	.10 (74,606) = 7,461	22,539	52,067
5	30,000	.10 (52,067) = 5,20724,793	27,274	
6	30,000	.10 (27,274) = 2,726*	27,274	0
	180,000	**36,276**	**143,724**	

* rounded

Sales-Type Lease – Lessor

A sales-type lease is different from a direct financing lease in only one respect. In a sales-type lease, the lessor receives a *manufacturer's or dealer's profit* on the "sale" of the asset in addition to the interest revenue earned over the lease term from financing the asset. The additional profit exists when the present value of the lease payments (the "sales price") exceeds the cost or carrying value of the asset "sold." A sales-type lease often occurs when a manufacturer or dealer uses leasing as a means of "selling" its product, rather than a leasing company serving as a lessor to finance the purchase of an asset by the lessee.

Accounting for a sales-type lease is precisely the same as for a direct financing lease except for recognizing the manufacturer's or dealer's profit at the inception of the sales-type lease. The profit is recorded, not as a single amount, but by recording both the sales revenue (the "sales price") and cost of goods sold (cost, that is, carrying value). Gross profit is the difference between sales revenue and cost of goods sold. We can modify the previous illustration to assume Lessee Company leased the equipment directly from the manufacturer.

Illustration

Manufacturing Company leased equipment to Lessee Company on January 1, 2003. Terms of the lease agreement were as follows:

Lease term: 6 years; 6 annual rent payments, payable at the beginning of each year.
Equipment's fair value: $143,724.
No residual value.
Lessor's required rate of return: 10%
Lessee's incremental borrowing rate: 10%
Manufacturing Company's cost to produce the equipment: : $100,000.

Sales-type lease?

"Selling price"	$143,724	
Lessor's cost	−100,000	
Lessor's profit	$ 43,724	**Yes**

Manufacturing Company's journal entries at the **inception of the lease** are:

Lease receivable (total payments: $30,000 x 6)	180,000	
Cost of goods sold (cost to lessor)..	100,000	
Sales revenue (present value of payments: $30,000 x 4.79079).......................		143,724
Unearned interest ($180,000 - 143,724)..		36,276
Asset (cost to lessor)		100,000
Cash..	30,000	
Lease receivable..		30,000

All entries other than the entry at the inception of the lease are the same for a sales-type lease and a direct financing lease. The amortization schedule is unaffected.

The lessee's accounting is not affected by how the lessor classifies the lease. All lessee entries are precisely the same as in the previous illustration of a direct financing lease.

PART B: RESIDUAL VALUE AND BARGAIN PURCHASE OPTIONS

Residual Value

A residual value for leased property is an estimate of what the asset's commercial value will be at the end of the lease term. If the *lessee* obtains title, the lessor's computation of rental payments is unaffected by any residual value. On the other hand, if the *lessor* retains title, the amount to be recovered through periodic lease payments is reduced by the present value of the residual amount.

For instance, if a leased asset has an estimated residual value of $50,000 at the end of a four-year lease, the lessor's cost (investment in the lease) is reduced by the present value of $50,000 to determine the amount that must be recovered from the lessee through periodic lease payments. If the asset's cost were $400,000, a lessor requiring a 10% rate of return on assets it finances would calculate annual lease payments due at the beginning of the year as follows:

$400,000	Lessor's investment to be recovered
(34,150)	Residual value ($50,000 x .68301 [PV of $1, n=4, i=10%])
$365,850	Amount to be recovered through periodic lease payments
÷ 3.48685	Present value of a $1 annuity due, n=4, i=10%
$104,923	Annual lease payments

Sometimes a lease agreement includes a guarantee by the lessee that the asset will have a specified residual value when custody of the asset reverts back to the lessor at the end of the lease term. A lessee-guaranteed residual value is considered by the lessee to be equivalent to an additional payment and thus is included in the calculation of the cost of the asset. In the example above, the lessee would calculate the amount to record as a leased asset and lease liability as:

$104,923	Annual lease payments
x 3.48685	Present value of a $1 annuity due, n=4, i=10%
$365,850	Present value of periodic lease payments
34,150	Present value of residual value ($50,000 x .68301 [PV of $1, n=4, i=10%])
$400,000	Leased asset and lease liability

On the other hand, if the lessee does not guarantee the residual value, the lessee's cost would simply be $365,850, the present value of periodic lease payments.

Bargain Purchase Option

A bargain purchase option (BPO) is included as a component of minimum lease payments for both the lessor and the lessee. Therefore, it's included in the calculations of both parties in precisely the same way as a lessee-guaranteed residual value. The lease term effectively ends when the BPO is exercisable.

PART C: OTHER LEASE ACCOUNTING ISSUES

Executory Costs

A responsibility of ownership that is transferred to the lessee in a capital lease is the responsibility to pay for maintenance, insurance, taxes, and any other costs usually associated with ownership. These costs are referred to as executory costs. The lessee simply expenses executory costs as incurred. As an expediency, sometimes a lease contract will specify that the lessor pays executory costs, but that the lessee will reimburse the lessor through higher rental payments. When rental payments are inflated for this reason, any portion of rental payments that represents executory costs is not considered part of minimum lease payments. They still are expensed by the lessee, even though paid through the lessor.

Initial Direct Costs

Any costs incurred by the lessor that are associated directly with originating a lease and are essential to acquire that lease are called initial direct costs. These costs include legal fees, commissions, evaluating the prospective lessee's financial condition, and preparing and processing lease documents. The method of accounting for initial direct costs depends on the nature of the lease. For *operating leases*, initial direct costs are recorded as assets and amortized over the term of the lease. For *direct financing leases*, interest revenue is earned over the lease term, so initial direct costs are matched with the interest revenues they help generate. For *sales-type leases*, initial direct costs are expensed at the inception of the lease.

Lease Disclosures

Financial statement disclosures in connection with leases include (a) a "general description" of the leasing arrangement as well as (b) minimum future payments, in the aggregate, and for each of the five succeeding fiscal years.

Decision-Makers' Perspective: Financial Statement Impact

Lease liabilities can affect the debt equity ratio as well as the rate of return on assets. Operating leases, too, represent long-term commitments that can become a problem if business declines and cash inflows drop off. The net income difference between treating a lease as a capital lease as opposed to an operating lease ordinarily is not significant, but the impact on the balance sheet between capital leases and operating leases is significant.

Lease payments (operating or nonoperating) are reported on a statement of cash flows as financing activities by the lessee and investing activities by the lessor. The primary difference between operating and nonoperating leases is that the lease at its inception would be reported as a non-cash investing/financing activity if treated as nonoperating, but not reported at all if treated as an operating lease.

PART D: SPECIAL LEASING ARRANGEMENTS

Sale-Leaseback Arrangement

In a sale-leaseback transaction the owner of an asset sells it and immediately leases it back from the new owner. A gain on the sale of an asset in a sale-leaseback arrangement is deferred and amortized over the lease term (or asset life if title is expected to transfer to the lessee). The lease portion of the transaction is evaluated and accounted for like any lease.

Real Estate Leases

Real estate leases involve land. Because land has an unlimited life only the first (title transfers) and second (BPO) classification criteria apply in a land lease. If the leased property includes both land and a building, neither of the first two criteria is met, and the fair value of the land is 25% or more of the combined fair value, then both the lessee and the lessor treat the land as an operating lease and the building as any other lease. The usual lease accounting treatment applies to leases that involve only part of a building even though some extra effort may be needed to arrive at reasonable estimates of cost and fair value.

Leveraged Leases

A leveraged lease involves significant long-term, nonrecourse financing by a third party creditor. The lessee accounts for a leveraged lease the same way as a nonleveraged lease. However, the lessor records its investment (receivable) net of the nonrecourse debt and reports income from the lease only in those years when the receivable exceeds the liability.

SELF-STUDY QUESTIONS AND EXERCISES

Concept Review

1. _____ leases are agreements that are formulated outwardly as leases, but that are in reality installment purchases.

2. Periodic interest expense is calculated by the lessee as the _____ interest rate times the amount of the outstanding lease liability during the period. The approach is the same regardless of the specific form of the debt – that is, whether in the form of notes, bonds, leases, pensions, or other debt instruments.

3. Conceptually, leases and _____ notes are accounted for in precisely the same way.

4. One criterion for a lease to classify as a capital lease is that the agreement specifies that _____ of the asset transfers to the lessee.

5. One criterion for a lease to classify as a capital lease is that the agreement contains a _____ option.

6. One criterion for a lease to classify as a capital lease is that the lease term is equal to _____ or more of the expected economic life of the asset.

7. One criterion for a lease to classify as a capital lease is that the present value of the minimum lease payments is equal to or greater than _____ of the fair value of the leased asset.

8. A bargain purchase option is a provision in the lease contract that gives the lessee the option of purchasing the leased property at a bargain price, defined as price sufficiently lower than the _____ of the property when the option becomes exercisable that the exercise of the option appears reasonably assured.

9. A _____ lease exists when the present value of the minimum lease payments exceeds the lessor's cost.

10. The minimum lease payments for the lessee should exclude any _____ not guaranteed by the lessee.

11. The minimum lease payments of the _____ includes any residual value not guaranteed by the lessee but guaranteed by a third-party guarantor.

12. Even when minimum lease payments are the same, their present values will differ if the lessee uses a discount rate different from the lessor's _____ .

13. The way a _____ is included in determining minimum lease payments is precisely the same way that a lessee-guaranteed residual value is included.

14. _____ are costs usually associated with ownership of an asset such as maintenance, insurance, and taxes.

15. When the lessor's implicit rate is unknown, the lessee should use its own _____ rate.

16. _____ rentals are *not* included in minimum lease payments but are reported in disclosure notes by both the lessor and lessee.

17. The costs of negotiating and consummating a completed lease transaction incurred by the lessor that are associated directly with originating a lease and are essential to acquire that lease are referred to as _____ . These include legal fees, evaluating the prospective lessee's financial condition, commissions, and preparing and processing lease documents.

18. In an _____ lease initial direct costs are recorded as prepaid expenses (assets) and amortized as an operating expense (usually straight-line) over the lease term.

19. In a _____ lease initial direct costs are amortized over the lease term, accomplished by offsetting unearned revenue by the initial direct costs.

20. In a _____ initial direct costs are expensed in the period of "sale" – that is, at the inception of the lease.

21. In a _____ the gain on the sale of the asset is not immediately recognized, but deferred and recognized over the term of the lease.

22. The FASB specifies exceptions to the general classification criteria for leases that involve _____ because of its unlimited useful life and the inexhaustibility of its inherent value through use.

23. A _____ lease involves significant long-term, nonrecourse financing by a third party creditor.

Answers:
1. Capital **2.** effective **3.** installment **4.** ownership **5.** bargain purchase **6.** 75% **7.** 90%
8. expected fair value **9.** sales-type **10.** residual value **11.** lessor **12.** implicit rate **13.** BPO
14. Executory costs **15.** incremental borrowing **16.** Contingent **17.** initial direct costs
18. operating **19.** direct financing **20.** sales-type lease **21.** sale-leaseback **22.** land
23. leveraged

REVIEW EXERCISES

Exercise 1

Electronic Leasing leases business equipment to consumers. On September 30, 2003, the company leased a computer to Transfer Services. The lease agreement specified quarterly payments of $400 beginning September 30, 2003, the inception of the lease, and each quarter (December 31, March 31, and June 30) through June 30, 2005 (two-year lease term). The estimated economic life of the computer is $2^{1}/_{2}$ years. Electronic Leasing's quarterly interest rate for determining payments was 3% (approximately 12% annually). Electronic Leasing paid $2,892 for the computer.

Required:

1. Calculate the cost of the computer to Transfer Services. [Be careful to note that, although payments occur on the last *calendar* day of each quarter, since the first payment was at the inception of the lease, payments represent an annuity due.] Round to nearest dollar. Show calculations.

2. Prepare the appropriate entries for Transfer Services on September 30, 2003. Round to nearest dollar. Show calculations.

3. Prepare the appropriate entries for Transfer Services on December 31, 2003. Round to nearest dollar. Show calculations.

Leases

Solution:

Cost:

Present value of quarterly rental payments ($400 x 7.23028**)		$2,892

** Present value of an annuity due of $1: n=8, i=3% (from Table 6A-6)

September 30, 2003

Leased asset (present value determined above).....................................	2,892	
Lease payable (lessor's cost)...		2,892
Lease payable (lease payment)...	400	
Cash (lease payment)		400

December 31, 2003

Interest expense (3% x [$2,892 - 400])....................................	75	
Lease payable (difference)	325	
Cash (lease payment)		400
Depreciation expense ($2,892 ÷ 8)	362	
Accumulated depreciation...		362

Exercise 2

Refer to the situation described in Exercise 1.

1. Show how Electronic Leasing determined the $400 lease payments.

2. Prepare the appropriate entries for Electronic Leasing on September 30, 2003. Round to nearest dollar. Show calculations.

3. Prepare the appropriate entries for Electronic Leasing on December 31, 2003. Round to nearest dollar. Show calculations.

Solution:

Quarterly rental payments :	$2,892	÷ 7.23028**	=	$400

** Present value of an annuity due of $1: n=8, i=3% (from Table 6A-6)

September 30, 2003

Lease receivable ($400 x 8).. 3,200

    Unearned interest revenue ($3,200 - 2,892) 308

    Inventory of equipment (lessor's cost) 2,892

Cash (lease payment)... 400

    Lease receivable 400

December 31, 2003

Cash (lease payment)... 400

    Lease receivable 400

Unearned interest revenue 75

    Interest revenue (3% x [$2,892 - 400]) 75

Exercise 3

Refer to the situation described in Exercise 1. Assume Transfer Services leased the computer directly from CCR Computer Company, which manufactured the computer at a cost of $2,000.

1. Calculate the dealer's profit to CCR Computer Company.

2. Prepare the appropriate entries for CCR Computer Company on September 30, 2003. Round to nearest dollar. Show calculations.

3. Prepare the appropriate entries for CCR Computer Company on December 31, 2003. Round to nearest dollar. Show calculations.

Leases

Solution:

Present value of quarterly rental payments ($400 x 7.23028**) $2,892

** Present value of an annuity due of $1: n=8, i=3% (from Table 6A-6)

"Selling price"	$2,892	
minus		
Computer's cost	(2,000)	
equals		
Dealer's profit	$ 892	

September 30, 2003

Lease receivable ($400 x 8)...	3,200	
Cost of goods sold (lessor's cost)...	2,000	
Sales revenue (calculated above)..		2,892
Unearned interest revenue ($3,200 - 2,892)...........................		308
Inventory of equipment (lessor's cost)...................................		2,000
Cash (lease payment)	400	
Lease receivable...		400

December 31, 2003

Cash (lease payment)	400	
Lease receivable...		400
Unearned interest revenue	75	
Interest revenue (3% x [$2,892 - 400]).................................		75

Exercise 4

Refer to the situation described in Exercises 1 and 2. Assume the computer has a residual value of $500 at the end of the two-year lease, but is not guaranteed by Transfer Services.

1. Calculate the lease payments that will allow Electronic Leasing to recover its $2,892 investment and achieve its desired rate of return.

2. Calculate the cost of the computer to Transfer Services.

Solution:

1. Quarterly rental payments : $2,892   -   ($500   x   .78941*)   = $2,497

* Present value of $1: n=8, i=3% (from Table 6A-2)

                                                           $2,497   ÷   7.23028**   = $345

** Present value of an annuity due of $1: n=8, i=3% (from Table 6A-6)

2. Cost:
Present value of quarterly rental payments ($345 x 7.23028**)$2,497

** Present value of an annuity due of $1: n=8, i=3% (from Table 6A-6)

Note: Because Transfer Services did not guarantee the residual value, the residual value is not considered a ninth
payment in the calculation.

MULTIPLE CHOICE

Enter the letter corresponding to the response that **best** completes each of the following statements or
questions.

____ 1.   Which of the following leases would least likely be classified as an operating lease by the
lessee?
   a.   The lease term is 5 years and the economic life of the leased asset is 8 years.
   b.   Ownership of the leased asset reverts to the lessor at the end of the lease term.
   c.   The agreement permits the lessee to buy the leased asset for one dollar at the end of
the lease term.
   d.   The fair value of the leased asset is $20 million and the present value of the lease
payments is $13 million.

____ 2.   Which of the following is not a sufficient criterion for a lessee to classify a lease as a
capital lease?
   a.   The lease transfers ownership of the leased asset to the lessee at the end of the lease
term.
   b.   The lessee has the option of acquiring the asset during or at the end of the lease term
at a bargain price.
   c.   The lease term is greater than two-thirds of the economic life of the asset.
   d.   The present value of the minimum lease payments is at least 90% of the fair value
of the leased asset.

_____ 3. For a lessor to consider a leasing arrangement to be a nonoperating lease, collectibility of the lease payments must be reasonably assured and:
   a. There must be no bargain purchase option.
   b. The lessee must be responsible for all executory costs over the term of the lease.
   c. The lease term must be 75% or more of the economic life of the asset.
   d. Any costs to the lessor yet to be incurred must be reasonably predictable.

_____ 4. In an operating lease in which the asset's economic life and lease term are different:
   a. The lessee depreciates the leased asset over the term of the lease.
   b. The lessor depreciates the leased asset over its economic life.
   c. The lessee should record a leased asset and a related obligation at the present value of the lease payments.
   d. The lessee depreciates the asset over its economic life.

_____ 5. If a capital lease contains a bargain purchase option, the lessee should depreciate the leased asset:
   a. Over the term of the lease.
   b. Without reference to the economic life of the asset.
   c. Over the economic life of the asset.
   d. Without reference to the term of the lease.

_____ 6. A necessary condition for a sales-type lease is:
   a. Legal title to the asset transfers to the lessee.
   b. The present value of minimum lease payments exceeds the lessor's cost.
   c. The lessor earns interest revenue instead of dealer's profit.
   d. The lessor earns dealer's profit instead of interest revenue.

_____ 7. The inception of a six-year capital lease is December 31, 2003. The agreement specifies equal annual lease payments on December 31 of each year. For the lessee, the first payment on December 31, 2003, includes:

	Interest Expense	Reduction of the Lease Liability
a.	No	Yes
b.	Yes	No
c.	Yes	Yes
d.	No	No

___ 8. Universal Leasing Corp. leases farm equipment to its customers under direct-financing leases. Typically the equipment has no residual value at the end of leases and the contracts call for payments at the beginning of each year. Universal's target rate of return is 10%. On a five-year lease of equipment with a fair value of $485,100, Universal will earn interest revenue over the life of the lease of:

    a. $ 96,575
    b. $114,900
    c. $121,275
    d. $194,040

___ 9. In a ten-year capital lease, the portion of the annual lease payment in the lease's third year that represents interest is:

    a.   The same as in the fourth year.
    b.   The same as in the first year.
    c.   Less than in the second year.
    d   More than in the second year.

___ 10. On January 1, 2003, Walter Scott Co. leased machinery under a 6-year lease. The machinery has a 9-year economic life. The present value of the monthly lease payments is determined to be 85% of the machinery's fair value. The lease contract includes neither a transfer of title to Scott nor a bargain purchase option. What amount should Scott report in its 2003 income statement?

    a.   Depreciation expense equal to one-ninth of the equipment's fair value.
    b.   Depreciation expense equal to one-sixth of the machinery's fair value.
    c.   Rent expense equal to the 2003 lease payments.
    d.   Rent expense equal to the 2003 lease payments minus interest.

___ 11. Pyramid Properties entered a lease that contains a bargain purchase option. When calculating the amount to capitalize as a leased asset at the inception of the lease term, the payment called for by the bargain purchase option should be:

    a.   Subtracted at its exercise price.
    b.   Subtracted at its present value.
    c.   Added at its present value.
    d.   Excluded from the calculation.

___ 12. Tucson Fruits leased farm equipment from Barr Machinery on July 1, 2003. The lease was recorded as a sales-type lease. The present value of the lease payments discounted at 10% was $40.5 million. Eight annual lease payments of $6 million are due at the beginning of each year beginning July 1, 2003. Barr had purchased the equipment for $33 million. What amount of interest revenue from the lease should Barr report in its 2003 income statement?

    a. $2,025,000
    b. $1,725,000
    c. $1,650,000
    d. $0

____ 13. On January 1, 2003, Jackson Properties leased a warehouse to Jensen Distributors. The operating lease provided for a nonrefundable bonus paid by Jensen. Jackson should recognize the bonus in earnings:
   a. At the inception of the lease.
   b. When the bonus is received.
   c. Over the life of the lease.
   d. At the expiration of the lease.

____ 14. Grant Industries leased exercise equipment to Silver Gyms on July 1, 2003. Grant recorded the lease as a sales-type lease at $810,000, the present value of minimum lease payments discounted at 10%. The lease called for eight annual lease payments of $120,000 due at the beginning of each year. The first payment was received on July 1, 2003. Grant had manufactured the equipment at a cost of $750,000. The total increase in earnings (pretax) on Grant's 2003 income statement would be:
   a. $0
   b. $93,000
   c. $94,500
   d. $100,500

____ 15. Brown Properties entered into a sale-leaseback transaction. Brown retains the right to substantially all of the remaining use of the property. A gain resulting from the sale should be:
   a. Reported as part of the asset's cost.
   b. Offset against losses from similar transactions.
   c. Deferred at the time of the sale-leaseback and subsequently amortized.
   d. Recognized in earnings at the time of the sale-leaseback.

Answers:

1.	c.	6.	b.	11.	c.
2.	c.	7.	a.	12.	b.
3.	d.	8.	a.	13.	c.
4.	b.	9.	c.	14.	c.
5.	c.	10.	c.	15.	c.

Chapter

16

Accounting for Income Taxes

LEARNING OBJECTIVES
After studying this chapter, you should be able to:
1. Describe the types of temporary differences that cause deferred tax liabilities and determine the amounts needed to record periodic income taxes.
2. Identify and describe the types of temporary differences that cause deferred tax assets.
3. Describe when and how a valuation allowance is recorded for deferred tax assets.
4. Explain why non-temporary differences have no deferred tax consequences.
5. Explain how a change in tax rates affects the measurement of deferred tax amounts.
6. Determine income tax amounts when multiple temporary differences exist.
7. Describe when and how an operating loss carryforward and an operating loss carryback are recognized in the financial statements.
8. Explain how deferred tax assets and deferred tax liabilities are classified and reported in a classified balance sheet and describe related disclosures.
9. Explain intraperiod tax allocation.

CHAPTER HIGHLIGHTS

PART A: DEFERRED TAX ASSETS AND DEFERRED TAX LIABILITIES

Temporary Differences

The revenues and expenses (and gains and losses) included on a company's income tax return usually are the same as those reported on the company's income statement for the same year. However, sometimes tax laws and financial accounting standards differ. One consequence of differences between GAAP and tax rules is that tax payments might occur in years different from when the revenues and expenses that cause the taxes are generated.

This situation produces differences between pretax *accounting* income and *taxable* income and, consequently, between the reported amount of an asset or liability in the financial statements and its tax basis. Such a difference is a temporary difference if it *originates* in one period and *reverses*, or "turns around," in one or more subsequent periods. An example would be income from installment sales in 2003 that is reported on the income statement in 2003 but is reported on the income tax

Accounting for Income Taxes

return when the installments are collected in 2004. Accounting income is higher than taxable income in 2003 when the difference originates.

Income Statement	Tax Return
Revenues (not including income from installment sales)	Revenues (not including income from installment sales)
Income from installment sales	
(Expenses)	(Expenses)
Accounting income	Taxable income

The temporary difference reverses, though, in 2004 when taxable income is higher than accounting income.

Income Statement	Tax Return
Revenues (not including income from installment sales)	Revenues (not including income from installment sales)
	Income from installment sales
(Expenses)	(Expenses)
Accounting income	Taxable income

Future Taxable Amounts (Deferred Tax Liabilities)

This temporary difference produces a future taxable amount because the taxable income will be increased relative to accounting income in 2004 when the difference reverses. Such differences produce *deferred tax liabilities* for the taxes to be paid on the future taxable amounts.

Income tax expense for a given year includes an amount for which payment (or receipt) is deferred in addition to the amount for which payment is due currently. That is, income tax expense includes both the current and deferred tax consequences of the activities of the reporting period.

Future taxable amounts are created by:

Revenues or gains reported on the tax return *after* the income statement:
➢ Installment sale income (installment method for taxes)
➢ Unrealized gain from recording investments at fair value (taxable when asset is sold)

Expenses or losses reported on the tax return *before* the income statement:
➢ Accelerated depreciation on the tax return (straight-line depreciation on the income statement)
➢ Prepaid expenses (tax-deductible when paid)
The most common cause of deferred tax liabilities is using accelerated depreciation on the tax return and straight-line depreciation on the income statement. The accelerated depreciation method permitted by tax law is the Modified Accelerated Cost Recovery System or MACRS. Here's an illustration:

Illustration

Diamond Industries purchased a delivery van for $40,000 on January 1, 2003. Diamond depreciates the van by the straight-line method over 4 years, assuming no residual value for financial reporting purposes. For tax purposes Diamond uses the MACRS, which mandates cost recovery at 25%, 38%, and 37% for each year of a 3-year recovery period. The resulting temporary differences are calculated as follows:

Year	Straight-line	MACRS	Temporary Differences	
2004	$10,000	$10,000	$ 0	
2005	10,000	15,200	5,200	(originating)
2006	10,000	14,800	4,800	(originating)
2007	10,000	–0–	(10,000)	(reversing)
	$40,000	$40,000	$ 0	

If we assume a 40% tax rate and no other differences between accounting income and taxable income, no deferred tax liability is created in 2004. In 2005, a deferred tax liability of $2,080 ($5,200 x 40%) is created by the 2005 temporary difference.

To see the effect over the life of the van, let's assume the following income statement for Diamond in 2005:

Revenues	$100,000
Operating expenses	(30,000)
Depreciation expense	(10,000)
Pretax accounting income	$60,000
Tax expense	?
Net income	?

From the table above, we can see that taxable income is $5,200 less than accounting income because depreciation for tax purposes is $5,200 higher than straight line. Tax expense can be calculated using the format used in the textbook as follows:

	Current Year 2005	Future Taxable Amounts		Future Taxable Amounts [total]
		2006	2007	
Accounting income	60,000			
Temporary difference:				
Depreciation	(5,200)	(4,800)	10,000	5,200
Taxable income	54,800			
Enacted tax rate	40%			40%
Tax payable currently	21,920			
Deferred tax liability				2,080
				↓

Deferred tax liability:	
Ending balance	$2,080
Less: Beginning balance	0
Change in balance	$2,080

Journal entry at the end of 2005

Income tax expense (to balance)	24,000	
Income tax payable (determined above)		21,920
Deferred tax liability (determined above)		2,080

Net income for Diamond in 2005:

Revenues	$100,000
Operating expenses	(30,000)
Depreciation expense	(10,000)
Pretax accounting income	$60,000
Tax expense	(24,000)
Net income	$36,000

The deferred tax liability increases in 2005 and 2006 (as the temporary difference originates) and is paid in 2007 (as the temporary difference reverses):

Deferred Tax Liability

		0	**2004**
		2,080	**2005** ($5,200 x 40%)
		1,920	**2006** ($4,800 x 40%)
2007 ($10,000 x 40%)	4,000		
		0	*balance after 4 years*

Future Deductible Amounts (Deferred Tax Assets)

When the future tax consequence of a temporary difference will be to *decrease* taxable income relative to accounting income *future deductible amounts* are created. These have favorable tax consequences that are recognized as deferred tax assets.

Future deductible amounts are created by:

Expenses or losses reported on the tax return *after* the income statement:
➤ Estimated expenses and losses (tax-deductible when paid)
➤ Unrealized loss from recording investments at fair value or inventory at LCM (tax-deductible when asset is sold)

Revenue or gains reported on the tax return *before* the income statement:
➤ Rent collected in advance
➤ Subscriptions collected in advance
➤ Other revenue collected in advance

Illustration

Golden-Detrich Corporation sells a product that carries a two-year warranty. The warranty expense was estimated for financial reporting purposes as $40,000 in 2004. For tax purposes, the expense is deducted when paid, evenly over the 2005-2006 period. The resulting temporary differences are calculated as follows:

Year	Warranty Expense	Tax Deduction	Temporary Differences	
2004	$40,000	0	$40,000	(originating)
2005	0	20,000	(20,000)	(reversing)
2006	0	20,000	(20,000)	(reversing)
	$40,000	$40,000	$ 0	

If we assume a 40% tax rate and no other differences between accounting income and taxable income, a deferred tax asset of $16,000 ($40,000 x 40%) is created by the 2004 temporary difference.

To see the effect over the three-year period, let's assume the following income statement for Diamond in 2004:

Revenues	$100,000
Operating expenses	(30,000)
Warranty expense	(40,000)
Pretax accounting income	$30,000
Tax expense	?
Net income	?

We can see that taxable income is $40,000 more than accounting income because warranty expense for tax purposes is $40,000 lower than warranty expense for financial reporting purposes. Tax expense can be calculated using the format used in the textbook as follows:

	Current Year 2004	Future Deductible Amounts 2005	Future Deductible Amounts 2006	Future Deductible Amounts [total]
Accounting income	30,000			
Temporary difference:				
Warranty expense	40,000	(20,000)	(20,000)	(40,000)
Taxable income	70,000			
Enacted tax rate	40%			40%
Tax payable currently	28,000			
Deferred tax asset				(16,000)
				↓

Deferred tax asset:

Ending balance	$16,000
Less: Beginning balance	0
Change in balance	$16,000

Journal entry at the end of 2004

Income tax expense (to balance)	12,000	
Deferred tax asset (determined above)	16,000	
Income tax payable (determined above)		28,000

Net income for Diamond in 2004:

Revenues	$100,000
Operating expenses	(30,000)
Warranty expense	(40,000)
Pretax accounting income	$30,000
Tax expense	(12,000)
Net income	$18,000

The deferred tax asset represents the future tax savings when the warranty expense becomes deductible. It is created in 2004 (as the temporary difference originates) and is realized in 2005 and 2006 (as the temporary difference reverses):

Deferred Tax Asset

2004 ($40,000 x 40%)	16,000		
		8,000	**2005** ($20,000 x 40%)
		8,000	**2006** ($20,000 x 40%)
balance after 3 years	0		

Valuation Allowance

Deferred tax assets are recognized for all deductible temporary differences. However, a deferred tax asset is then reduced by a valuation allowance if it is "more likely than not" that some portion or all of the deferred tax asset will not be realized.

For example, let's say that in the previous illustration management determines in 2004 that it's more likely than not that $6,000 of the deferred tax asset will not ultimately be realized because income in 2005 and 2006 is not expected to be more than the available tax deduction. The deferred tax asset would be reduced by the creation of a valuation allowance as follows:

Income tax expense	6,000	
Valuation allowance – deferred tax asset		6,000

The effect is to increase the income tax expense as a result of reduced expectations of future tax savings. On the 2004 balance sheet, the deferred tax asset would be reported at its estimated net realizable value:

Deferred tax asset	$16,000
Less: Valuation allowance – deferred tax asset	6,000
	$10,000

Non-Temporary Differences

Non-temporary differences, or permanent differences, are those caused by transactions and events that under existing tax law will never affect taxable income or taxes payable. An example is interest received from investments in bonds issued by state and municipal governments. This income is exempt from taxation. Interest revenue of this type is reported as revenue on the income statement, but not on the tax return. As a result, accounting income exceeds taxable income. Unlike for a temporary difference, this situation will not reverse in a later year. Taxable income in a later year will not exceed accounting income because the tax-free income will never be reported on the tax return. Permanent differences are disregarded when determining both the tax payable currently and the deferred tax effect.

Examples of permanent differences are:

> ➤ Interest received from investments in bonds issued by state and municipal governments (not taxable).
> ➤ Investment expenses incurred to obtain tax-exempt income (not tax deductible).
> ➤ Life insurance proceeds upon the death of an insured executive (not taxable).
> ➤ Premiums paid for life insurance policies when the payer is the beneficiary (not tax deductible).
> ➤ Compensation expense pertaining to some employee stock option plans (not tax deductible).
> ➤ Expenses due to violations of the law (not tax deductible).
> ➤ Portion of dividends received from U.S. corporations that is not taxable due to the "dividends received deduction."
> ➤ Tax deduction for depletion of natural resources (percentage depletion) that permanently exceeds the income statement depletion expense (cost depletion).
> ➤ Tax deduction for goodwill amortization over 15 years (goodwill is not amortized for financial reporting purposes).

PART B: OTHER TAX ACCOUNTING ISSUES

Change in Tax Rates

The deferred tax liability or asset is based on currently enacted tax rates and laws applied to the taxable or deductible amounts rather than anticipated tax rates. When a phased-in change in rates is scheduled to occur, the specific tax rates of each future year are multiplied by the amounts reversing in each of those years. The total is the deferred tax liability or asset. For instance, in our previous illustration, let's say the tax rate is 40% in 2004 but is scheduled to become 35% in 2006, our calculation in 2004 would be modified as follows:

	Current Year 2004	Future deductible Amounts		[total]
		2005	2006	
Accounting income	30,000			
Temporary difference:				
Warranty expense	40,000	(20,000)	(20,000)	
Taxable income	70,000			
Enacted tax rate	40%	40%	35%	
Tax payable currently	28,000			
Deferred tax asset		8,000	7,000	15,000
				↓

Deferred tax asset:	
Ending balance	$15,000
Less: Beginning balance	0
Change in balance	$15,000

Journal entry at the end of 2004		
Income tax expense (to balance)	13,000	
Deferred tax asset (determined above)	15,000	
Income tax payable (determined above)		28,000

If a change in a tax law or rate occurs, the deferred tax liability or asset is adjusted to reflect the change in the amount to be paid or recovered. The effect of the adjustment is reflected in operating income in the year of the tax law or rate change.

Multiple Temporary Differences

Normally, a company will have several temporary differences both originating and reversing in any given year. When multiple temporary differences exist, our approach does not change. We focus on total amounts rather than individual amounts. The total of the future taxable amounts is multiplied by the future tax rate to determine the appropriate balance for the deferred tax liability, and the total of the future deductible amounts is multiplied by the future tax rate to determine the appropriate balance for the deferred tax asset.

Net Operating Losses

Tax laws allow an operating loss to be used to reduce taxable income in other, profitable years by either a carryback of the loss to prior years (2 years) or a carryforward of the loss to later years (up to 20 years). The income tax benefit of both an operating loss carryback and an operating loss carryforward are recognized for accounting purposes in the year the operating loss occurs. The net *after-tax* operating loss reflects the reduction of past taxes from the loss carryback and future tax savings that the loss carryforward is expected to create.

Illustration

During 2004, Midsouth Cellular Corporation reported an operating loss of $135,000 for financial reporting and tax purposes. The company's enacted tax rate is 40%. Taxable income, tax rates, and income taxes paid in three previous years were as follows:

	Taxable Income	Tax Rates	Income Taxes Paid
2001	$40,000	45%	$18,000
2002	80,000	40%	32,000
2003	30,000	40%	12,000

Here's how the income tax benefit of the operating loss carryback and the operating loss carryforward is determined:

($ in 000s)	Prior Years 2002	2003	Current Year 2004	Future Deductible Amounts [total]
Operating loss			(135)	
Loss carryback	(80)	(30)	110	
Loss carryforward			25	(25)
			0	
Enacted tax rate	40%	40%	40%	40%
Tax payable (refundable)	(32)	(12)	0	
Deferred tax asset				(10)

Journal entry at the end of 2004

Receivable – income tax refund ($32 + 12)	44	
Deferred tax asset (determined above)	10	
Income tax benefit – operating loss (to balance)		54

Financial Statement Presentation

Deferred tax assets and deferred tax liabilities are classified as either current or noncurrent depending on how the related assets or liabilities are classified for financial reporting. A net current amount and a net noncurrent amount are reported as either an asset or a liability.

Disclosure notes should report additional relevant information needed for full disclosure pertaining to deferred tax amounts reported on the balance sheet, the components of income tax expense, and available operating loss carryforwards.

Intraperiod Tax Allocation

Through intraperiod tax allocation the total income tax expense for a reporting period is allocated among the financial statement items that gave rise to it. As a result, each of the following items should be reported net of its respective income tax effects:

- Income (or loss) from continuing operations
- Discontinued operations
- Extraordinary items
- Changes in accounting principle
- Prior period adjustments (to the beginning retained earnings balance)

Decision-Makers' Perspective

Those who make decisions based on estimated pre-tax numbers are perilously ignoring one of the most important aspects of those decisions. As one of the largest expenditures that many firms incur, income tax is a key element in any decision that managers and external analysts make. Managers and other decision-makers should constantly be alert to choices that minimize or delay taxes.

Investment patterns in a statement of cash flows and other disclosures can indicate potential tax expenditures. Significant investments in buildings and equipment can signify deferred tax liabilities from temporary differences in depreciation. New investments that cause the level of depreciable assets to at least remain constant over time can effectively delay that deferred tax liability indefinitely. Analysts should be alert to situations such as impending plant closings or investment patterns that suggest declining levels of depreciable assets and therefore might cause material paydowns of that deferred tax liability.

Deferred tax assets represent future tax savings. In particular, a deferred tax asset that often reflects sizable future tax deductions is an operating loss carryforward. Operating loss carryforwards can indicate significant future tax benefits because they allow large amounts of future income to be earned tax-free. Analysts should not overlook this potentially generous tax shelter.

Increasing debt increases risk. Because deferred tax liabilities increase reported debt, deferred tax liabilities increase risk as measured by the debt to equity ratio.

Accounting for Income Taxes

SELF-STUDY QUESTIONS AND EXERCISES

Concept Review

1. _____ is comprised of both the *current* and the *deferred* tax consequences of events and transactions already recognized.

2. Income tax expense includes (a) the income tax that is payable _____ and (b) the change in the _____ tax liability (or asset).

3. _____ between the reported amount of an asset or liability in the financial statements and its tax basis are primarily caused by revenues, expenses, gains, and losses being included in taxable income in a year earlier or later than the year in which they are recognized for financial reporting purpose.

4. Some temporary differences create deferred tax _____ because they result in taxable amounts in some future year(s) when the related assets are recovered or the related liabilities are settled (when the temporary differences reverse).

5. Some temporary differences create deferred tax _____ because they result in deductible amounts in some future year(s) when the related assets are recovered or the related liabilities are settled (when the temporary differences reverse).

6. Estimated warranty expense is recognized for _____ . The warranty cost is then deducted for _____ when paid.

7. Future deductible amounts mean that taxable income will be _____ relative to accounting income in one or more future years.

8. Two examples of future _____ amounts are (a) estimated expenses that are recognized on income statements when incurred, but deducted on tax returns in later years when actually paid and (b) revenues that are taxed when collected, but are recognized on income statements in later years when actually earned.

9. A deferred tax asset is reduced by a _____ if it is "more likely than not" that some portion or all of the deferred tax asset will not be realized.

10. _____ differences are caused by transactions and events that under existing tax law will never affect taxable income or taxes payable. These are disregarded when determining both the tax payable currently and the deferred tax effect.

11. Interest received from investments in bonds issued by _____ is not taxable.

12. Investment expenses incurred to obtain _____ income is not tax deductible.

13. When determining a deferred tax asset or liability, a company should use the currently enacted tax rate that will be effective in the year(s) a temporary difference _____ .

14. When a change in a tax law or rate occurs, a deferred tax liability or asset must be adjusted to reflect the amount to be paid or recovered in the future. The effect is reflected in operating income (adjustment to income tax expense) in the year of _____ .

15. The income tax benefit of either an operating loss carryback or an operating loss carryforward is recognized for accounting purposes in the year _____ .

16. The net after-tax operating loss reflects the reduction of past taxes from the loss _____ or future tax savings that the loss _____ is expected to create.

17. An operating loss carryforward creates future _____ amounts, so a deferred tax _____ is recognized for an operating loss carryforward.

18. Deferred tax assets and deferred tax liabilities are not reported individually, but combined instead into a net _____ amount and a net _____ amount. Each is reported as either an asset – if deferred tax assets exceed deferred tax liabilities, or as a liability – if deferred tax liabilities exceed deferred tax assets.

19. Deferred tax assets and deferred tax liabilities are classified as either *current* or *noncurrent* according to how _____ .

20. Regarding deferred tax amounts reported on the balance sheet, disclosure notes should indicate (a) the total of all deferred tax _____ , (b) the total of all deferred tax _____ , (c) the total _____ recognized for deferred tax assets, (d) the net change in the _____ , and (e) the approximate tax effect of each type of temporary difference (and carryforward).

21. Pertaining to the income tax expense reported on the income statement, disclosure notes should indicate (a) the _____ portion of the tax expense (or tax benefit), (b) the _____ portion of the tax expense (or tax benefit), with separate disclosure of amounts attributable to (c) the portion that does not include the effect of the following separately disclosed amounts, (d) operating loss carryforwards, (e) adjustments due to changes in tax laws or rates, (e) adjustments to the beginning-of-the-year valuation allowance due to revised estimates, (f) investment tax credits.

22. _____ tax allocation means the total income tax expense for a reporting period is allocated among the financial statement items that gave rise to the income tax expense.

Answers:

1. Income tax expense **2.** currently; deferred **3.** Temporary differences **4.** liabilities
5. assets **6.** financial reporting; tax purposes **7.** decreased **8.** deductible **9.** valuation allowance **10.**
Non-temporary or "permanent" **11.** state and municipal governments
12. tax-exempt **13.** reverses **14.** the enactment of the change in the tax law or rate.
15. the operating loss occurs. **16.** carryback, carryforward **17.** deductible, asset
18. current, noncurrent **19.** the related assets or liabilities are classified for financial reporting **20.**
liabilities, assets, valuation allowance, valuation allowance **21.** current, deferred **22.** Intraperiod

REVIEW EXERCISES

Exercise 1

At December 31, 2004, the account balances of American Transport, a national distribution firm, included income taxes payable of $570,000. Also, a current deferred tax asset of $900,000 was calculated based on future deductible amounts. The previous year's financial statements reported a current deferred tax asset of $600,000 with a valuation allowance of $30,000. At December 31, 2004, it was determined that it was more likely than not that 10% of the deferred tax asset ultimately would not be realized. American Transport had made no estimated tax payments during 2004.

Required:

1. Determine the current portion of American Transport's income tax expense.

2. Determine the deferred portion of American Transport's income tax expense.

3. Determine the appropriate valuation allowance, if any, to report on American Transport's 2004 balance sheet.

4. Determine the appropriate change in the valuation allowance, if any, to record at the end of 2004.

5. Prepare the appropriate journal entry to record American Transport's 2004 income taxes.

Accounting for Income Taxes

Solution:

Requirement 1

       Income tax payable (given)   <u>$570,000</u>

Requirement 2

$900,000 current deferred tax asset
<u>(600,000)</u> previous deferred tax asset
<u>$300,000</u> increase in deferred tax asset

Requirement 3

$900,000   current deferred tax asset
<u>x   10%</u>   percentage estimated not to be realized
$ 90,000   valuation allowance

Requirement 4

$ 90,000   new valuation allowance
<u> (30,000)</u>   previous valuation allowance
<u>$ 60,000</u>   increase in valuation allowance

Requirement 5

Income tax expense (to balance)	330,000	
Deferred tax asset (determined above)	300,000	
Valuation allowance (determined above)		60,000
Income tax payable (given)		570,000

Exercise 2

Boston Developers sells some of its properties on an installment basis. For these sales, Boston recognizes installment income for financial reporting purposes in the year of the sale, but for tax purposes, installment income is reported by the installment method. 2003 installment income was $1,800,000 and will be collected over the next three years as follows:

2004	$450,000
2005	750,000
2006	600,000

The tax rate is 30%, but based on an enacted law, is scheduled to become 40% in 2005.

Boston began operations in 2003 and its pretax *accounting* income for 2003 was $2,430,000. This includes interest revenue of $30,000 from municipal bonds. There were no differences between accounting income and taxable income other than those described above.

Required:

1. Prepare the appropriate journal entry to record Boston's 2003 income taxes.

2. What is Boston's 2003 net income?

Accounting for Income Taxes

Solution:

1. ($ in thousands)

	Current Year 2003	Future Taxable Amounts		
		2004	2005	2006
Accounting income	2,430			
Non-temporary difference	(30)			
Temporary difference:				
Installment sales	(1,800)	450	750	600
Taxable income	600			
Enacted tax rate	30%	30%	40%	40%
Tax payable currently	**180**			
Deferred tax liability		135	300	240	675

Less: beginning balance:	0
Change in balance: credit (debit)	**675**

Journal entry at the end of 2003

Income tax expense (to balance)	855	
Deferred tax liability (determined above)		675
Income tax payable (determined above)		180

2. ($ in thousands)

Pretax accounting income	$2,430
Income tax expense	(855)
Net income	$1,575

MULTIPLE CHOICE

Enter the letter corresponding to the response that **best** completes each of the following statements or questions.

____ 1. Temporary differences arise when expenses are reported in the income statement:

	After they are deductible for tax purposes	Before they are deductible for tax purposes
a.	Yes	Yes
b.	Yes	No
c.	No	No
d.	No	Yes

© *The McGraw-Hill Companies, Inc., 2004*

16-18   *Intermediate Accounting, 3/e*

_____ 2. Brown and Lowery, Inc. reported $470 million in income before income taxes for 2003, its first year of operations. Tax depreciation exceeded depreciation for financial reporting purposes by $50 million. The firm also had non-tax-deductible expenses of $20 million relating to non-temporary differences. The income tax rate for 2003 was 35%, but the enacted rate for years after 2003 is 40%. The balance in the deferred tax liability in the December 31, 2003, balance sheet is:
   a. $ 8.0 million
   b. $17.5 million
   c. $20.0 million
   d. $28.0 million

_____ 3. At December 31, 2003, the account balances of Dowling, Inc. showed income taxes payable of $38 million and a current deferred tax asset of $60 million before assessing the need for a valuation allowance. The previous year Dowling had reported a current deferred tax asset of $45 million with no valuation allowance. Dowling determined that it was more likely than not that 20% of the deferred tax asset ultimately would not be realized. Dowling made no estimated tax payments during 2003. What amount should Dowling report as total income tax expense in its 2003 income statement?
   a. $12 million.
   b. $23 million.
   c. $35 million.
   d. $38 million.

_____ 4. The financial reporting carrying amount of Johns-Hopper Company's only depreciable asset exceeded its tax basis by $750,000 at December 31, 2003. This was a result of differences between depreciation for financial reporting purposes and tax purposes. The asset was acquired earlier in the year. Johns-Hopper has no other temporary differences. The enacted tax rate is 30% for 2003 and 40% thereafter. Johns-Hopper should report the deferred tax effect of this difference in its December 31, 2003, balance sheet as:
   a. A liability of $ 225,000.
   b. A liability of $300,000.
   c. An asset of $ 225,000.
   d. An asset of $300,000.

_____ 5. Pretax financial statement income for the year ended December 31, 2003, was $25 million for Scott Pen Company. Scott's taxable income was $30 million. This was a result of differences between depreciation for financial reporting purposes and tax purposes. The enacted tax rate is 30% for 2003 and 40% thereafter. What amount should Scott report as the **current** portion of income tax expense for 2003?
    a. $7.5 million
    b. $ 9 million
    c. $ 10 million
    d. $ 12 million

Questions 6 – 9 are based on the following:

A reconciliation of pretax financial statement income to taxable income is shown below for Shaw-Anderson Industries for the year ended December 31, 2003, its first year of operations. The income tax rate is 40%.

Pretax accounting income	$640,000
Interest revenue on municipal securities	(20,000)
Warranty expense in excess of deductible amount	45,000
Depreciation in excess of financial statement amount	(120,000)
Taxable income	$545,000

_____ 6. What amount should Shaw-Anderson report as the **current** portion of income tax expense on its 2003 income statement?
    a. $52,000
    b. $218,000
    c. $248,000
    d. $256,000

_____ 7. What amount should Shaw-Anderson report as the **deferred** portion of income tax expense on its 2003 income statement?
    a. $18,000
    b. $30,000
    c. $38,000
    d. $56,000

_____ 8. What amount should Shaw-Anderson report as a current item related to deferred income taxes on its 2003 balance sheet?
    a. Deferred income tax liability of $18,000.
    b. Deferred income tax liability of $30,000.
    c. Deferred income tax asset of $18,000.
    d. Deferred income tax asset of $30,000.

_____ 9. What amount should Shaw-Anderson report as a noncurrent item related to deferred income taxes on its 2003 balance sheet?
    a. Deferred income tax liability of $30,000.
    b. Deferred income tax liability of $48,000.
    c. Deferred income tax asset of $30,000.
    d. Deferred income tax asset of $48,000.

____ 10. The pretax financial statement income for Yeager Industries was $32 million the year ended December 31, 2003. Yeager's taxable income was $25 million. The difference was due to differences between depreciation for financial reporting purposes and tax purposes. The enacted tax rate is 40% for 2003 and 35% thereafter. If no 2003 taxes have been paid, what is Yeager's current liability for income taxes for 2003?
   a. $12.8 million
   b. $10.0 million
   c. $11.2 million
   d. $ 8.7 million

____ 11. Easterwood Motors reported a net deferred tax liability of $45,000 and pretax financial statement income of $1,500,000 in its December 31, 2002, financial statements. Taxable income was $1,000,000 for 2003. At December 31, 2003, Easterwood had cumulative deductible differences of $350,000. Easterwood's effective income tax rate is 40%. What should Easterwood report as the **deferred** portion of income tax expense on its December 31, 2003, income statement?
   a. $140,000
   b. $158,000
   c. $185,000
   d. $400,000

____ 12. In its first three years of operations Jenkins Productions reported the following operating income (loss) amounts:

2001	$ 450,000
2002	(1,050,000)
2003	1,800,000

There were no deferred income taxes in any year. In 2002, Jenkins elected to carry back its operating loss. The enacted income tax rate was 35% in 2001 and 40% thereafter. In its 2003 balance sheet, what amount should Jenkins report as current income tax payable?
   a. $300,000
   b. $420,000
   c. $480,000
   d. $720,000

___ 13. In its first four years of operations Cordelli Resorts reported the following operating income (loss) amounts:

2000	$300,000
2001	200,000
2002	(850,000)
2003	900,000

There were no other deferred income taxes in any year. In 2002, Cordelli elected to carry back its operating loss. The enacted income tax rate was 40%. In its 2003 income statement, what amount should Cordelli report as income tax expense?
a. $160,000
b. $220,000
c. $340,000
d. $360,000

___ 14. At December 31, 2003, Control Enterprises had the following deferred income tax items:

Deferred income tax liability of $24 million related to a current asset
Deferred income tax asset of $18 million related to a current liability
Deferred income tax liability of $40 million related to a noncurrent asset
Deferred income tax asset of $12 million related to a noncurrent liability

Control Enterprises should report in the current section of its December 31, 2003, balance sheet a:
a. Noncurrent asset of $30,000 and a non-current liability of $64,000.
b. Current asset of $6,000.
c. Noncurrent asset of $28,000 and a non-current liability of $15,000.
d. Noncurrent liability of $10,000.

___ 15. Using straight-line depreciation for financial reporting purposes and MACRS for tax purposes creates a:
a. A temporary difference requiring intraperiod tax allocation.
b. A permanent difference not requiring interperiod tax allocation.
c. Deferred tax asset.
d. A deferred tax liability.

____ 16.   List Corporation reported pretax accounting income of $90,000, but due to temporary differences, taxable income is only $50,000. Assuming a tax rate of 40%, the income statement should report net income of:
   a. $16,000
   b. $20,000
   c. $36,000
   d. $54,000

____ 17.   The income tax benefit of an operating loss carryforward is recognized in the year the loss occurs:
   a.   Unless it's more likely than not that the future tax savings will not be realized.
   b.   Unless there is no taxable income in the two previous years.
   c.   When the loss year is the company's first year of operations.
   d.   Always.

____ 18.   Typically, the tax effects of an operating loss carryback are:
   a.   Not reported on the income statement.
   b.   Recognized in the period(s) the benefits are realized.
   c.   Deferred and amortized over 15 years.
   d.   Recognized in the year the loss occurs.

Answers:

1.	a.	6.	b.	11.	c.	16.	d.
2.	c.	7.	b.	12.	c.	17.	a.
3.	c.	8.	c.	13.	d.	18.	d.
4.	b.	9.	b.	14.	b.		
5.	b.	10.	b.	15.	d.		

Pensions

LEARNING OBJECTIVES

After studying this chapter, you should be able to:

1. Explain the fundamental differences between a *defined contribution* pension plan and a *defined benefit* pension plan.
2. Distinguish among the *accumulated* benefit obligation, the *vested* benefit obligation, and the *projected* benefit obligation.
3. Describe the five events that might change the balance of the PBO.
4. Explain how plan assets accumulate to provide retiree benefits and understand the role of the trustee in administering the fund.
5. Describe how pension expense is a composite of periodic changes that occur in both the pension obligation and the plan assets.
6. Understand the interrelationships among the elements that constitute a defined benefit pension plan.
7. Describe how pension disclosures fill a reporting gap left by the minimal disclosures in the primary financial statements.

CHAPTER HIGHLIGHTS

PART A – THE NATURE OF PENSION PLANS

Types of Pension Plans

Pension plans are designed to provide income to individuals during their retirement years. By setting aside funds during an employee's working years, at retirement, the accumulated funds plus earnings from investing those funds are available to replace wages. There are two basic types of pension plans:

⇨ **Defined contribution pension plans**

These promise fixed annual contributions to a pension fund (3% of employees' pay, for instance). The employee chooses where funds are invested. Designated options usually include stocks or fixed-income securities. Retirement pay depends on the accumulated balance of the fund at retirement.

⇨ **Defined benefit pension plans**

These promise fixed retirement benefits "defined" by a pension formula. Normally, the pension formula bases retirement pay on the employees' (a) years of service, (b) annual compensation [often final pay or an average for the last few years], and sometimes (c) age. The employer company is responsible for ensuring that sufficient funds are available to provide promised benefits.

Each type of plan has the same objective, which is to provide income to employees during their retirement years. However, they differ regarding who bears the risk of ensuring that the objective is achieved.

Defined Contribution Plans

Defined contribution plans promise defined periodic contributions to a pension fund, without further commitment regarding benefit amounts at retirement. Retirement benefits are entirely dependent upon how well investments perform. Thus, the employee bears the risk of uncertain investment returns. The employer is free of any further obligation.

These plans have several variations, the most common being 401(k) plans – named after the Tax Code section which specifies the conditions for the favorable tax treatment of these plans. 401(k) plans allow voluntary contributions by employees, which often are matched to a specified extent by employers. The employer simply records pension expense equal to the cash contribution:

Pension expense...	<contribution>
Cash	<contribution>

Defined Benefit Plans

Defined benefit plans promise fixed retirement benefits "defined" by a designated pension formula. A typical pension formula will specify that a retiree will receive annual retirement benefits based on the employee's years of service and annual pay at retirement. For instance, a pension formula could define annual retirement benefits as:

2% x years of service x average salary last three years

If this were the formula, the annual retirement benefits to an employee who retires after 25 years of service, with an average salary of $80,000 for the three years prior to retirement, would be:

2% x 25 years x $80,000 = $40,000

The fundamental components of a defined benefit pension plan are:

⇨ The employer's obligation to pay retirement benefits in the future.

⇨ The plan assets set aside by the employer from which to pay the retirement benefits in the future.

⇨ The periodic expense of having a pension plan.

The first two of these, the employer's obligation and plan assets, are not included on a company's primary financial statements, but are reported in disclosure notes. The third, pension expense, is reported on the income statement. The pension expense is comprised of several elements that include changes the employer's obligation and plan assets, so we discuss those first before looking at the components of pension expense.

PART B: THE PENSION OBLIGATION AND PLAN ASSETS

The Pension Obligation

There are three different ways to measure the pension obligation:

⇨ **Accumulated Benefit Obligation (ABO)** – present value of estimated retirement benefits earned so far by employees, estimated by plugging *existing* compensation levels into the pension formula.

⇨ **Vested Benefit Obligation (VBO)** - vested portion of the accumulated benefit obligation – part that plan participants are entitled to receive *regardless of their continued employment*.

⇨ **Projected Benefit Obligation (PBO)** – present value of estimated retirement benefits earned so far by employees, estimated by plugging *projected* compensation levels into the pension formula.

Remember, these are three ways to measure the same liability. Typically, a company hires an actuary to make these estimates. The accountants then report the liability in disclosure notes and also use changes in the liability as part of the calculation of the pension expense.

The PBO can change for the following reasons:

PBO at the *beginning* of the year

⇨   **Prior service cost** - cost of making plan amendments retroactive to prior years

⇨   **Service cost** - increase in the PBO attributable to employee service this year

⇨   **Interest cost** - accrual of interest as time passes (beginning PBO x discount rate)

⇨   **Loss (gain) on PBO** - periodic adjustments to PBO when estimates change

⇨   **Less: Retiree benefits paid** - benefits actually paid to retired employees

PBO at the *end* of the year

The PBO may never be affected by prior service cost. When a pension plan is amended, credit often is given for employee service rendered in prior years. The cost of doing so is called prior service cost. If a pension plan never is amended, this increase in the PBO will not occur. On the other hand, the service cost, interest cost, payment of benefits occur each period. Losses and gains also occur frequently because changes occur frequently in various estimates used to calculate the liability.

The Plan Assets

Funds accumulated to pay the pension obligation are the plan assets. A trustee accepts employer contributions, invests the contributions, accumulates the earnings on the investments, and pays benefits from the plan assets to retired employees or their beneficiaries. The trustee invests plan assets in stocks, bonds, and other income producing assets. The accumulated balance of the contributions plus the return on the investments is anticipated to be sufficient to pay benefits as they come due.

Similar to the PBO, the balance in pension plan assets is not formally recognized on the balance sheet, but is actively monitored in the employer's informal records. The trustee reports to the employer the changes in assets of a pension fund, which include the following:

Plan assets at the *beginning* of the year

⇨ **Return on plan assets** - dividends, interest, market price appreciation

⇨ **Cash contributions** - employer contributions

⇨ **Less: Retiree benefits paid** - benefits actually paid to retired employees

Plan assets at the *end* of the year

PART C: DETERMINING PENSION EXPENSE

Even though employees receive pension benefits long after they earn those benefits, the employer's cost of providing those benefits is allocated to the periods the services are performed. The periodic pension expense is a composite of periodic changes in both the pension obligation and the plan assets. Specifically, pension expense includes:

⇨ **Service cost** - increase in the PBO attributable to employee service this year

⇨ **Interest cost** - accrual of interest as time passes (beginning PBO x discount rate)

⇨ **Actual return on the plan assets** - dividends, interest, price appreciation

   Adjusted for: loss or gain - difference between actual and expected return

⇨ **Amortization of prior service cost**

⇨ **Amortization of the net loss or net gain**

   Pension expense

Illustration

Actuary and trustee reports indicate the following changes in the PBO and plan assets of GT&T Cellular during 2003:

Prior service cost from plan amendment at the beginning of 2003	$26 million
Unrecognized net gain at Jan.1, 2003 (previous gains exceeded previous losses)	$25 million
Average remaining service life of the active employee group	13 years
Actuary's discount rate	5%

($ in millions)	PBO		PLAN ASSETS
Beginning of 2003	$120	*Beginning* of 2003	$100
Service cost	13	Return on plan assets,	
Interest cost, 5%	6	5% (7% expected)	5
Loss (gain) on PBO	(1)	Cash contributions	9
Less: Retiree benefits	(10)	Less: Retiree benefits	(10)
End of 2003	$128	*End* of 2003	$104

Pensions

Calculation of pension expense: ($ in millions)

Service cost (from PBO above)	$13
Interest cost (from PBO above)	6
Actual return on the plan assets (from Plan Assets above)	$5
Adjusted for: loss on the plan assets ([7% - 5%] x $100)	2
Expected return on the plan assets	(7)
Amortization of prior service cost ($26 / 13 years)	2
Amortization of the net gain*	(1)
Pension expense	**$13**

* Amortization of the net gain:

	($ in millions)
Net gain (previous gains exceeded previous losses)	$25
10% of $120 ($120 is greater than $100): the "corridor"	12
Excess at the beginning of the year	$13
Average remaining service period	÷ 13 years
Amount amortized to 2003 pension expense	**$1**

The service cost is the increase in the PBO attributable to employee service and is the primary component of pension expense.

The interest and return-on-assets components are "financial items" created only because the compensation is delayed and the obligation is funded currently. Notice that the actual return on assets is increased by the loss on plan assets so that effectively the expected return is the component of pension expense. This is due to the desire to achieve income smoothing by delaying the recognition of both the loss (gain) on the PBO and the loss (gain) on plan assets. If gains and losses were immediately recognized in pension expense, the annual pension expense and therefore income would rise and fall frequently with each difference between results and expectations.

By the straight-line method, prior service cost is recognized over the average remaining service life of the active employee group.

Delaying the recognition of both the loss (gain) on the PBO and the loss (gain) on plan assets means these amounts are set aside for possible future recognition. If and when a net gain or net loss gets "too large" a portion of the excess is included in pension expense. The amount included is the excess divided by the average remaining service life of the active employee group. Too large is defined by the FASB as greater than 10% of either plan assets or the PBO (at the beginning of the year), whichever is larger. Since the net gain ($25 million) exceeds an amount equal to the greater of 10% of the PBO or 10% of plan assets ($12 million), part of the $13 million excess is amortized to pension expense.

Recording the Periodic Expense and Periodic Funding

The measurement of the periodic pension expense and the funding of the pension plan are two separate determinations, motivated by different decisions. Pension expense is an *accounting* decision, whereas how much cash to contribute each year is a *financing* decision affected by cash flow and tax considerations, as well as minimum funding requirements of ERISA. Taking these considerations into account, employers calculate cash contributions with the objective of accumulating sufficient funds (contributions plus investment returns) to provide promised retirement benefits to retired employees. As a result, the debit to pension expense and the credit to cash rarely will be the same.

In our illustration above, the following journal entry would be made by GT&T Cellular in 2003 to record both the annual pension expense and the annual contribution to the pension fund:

	($ in millions)	
Pension expense (calculated above)............................	13	
Prepaid (accrued) pension cost (difference)		4
Cash (contribution to fund)....................................		9

We use a single account "prepaid (accrued) pension cost" to record the difference between pension expense and the cash contribution to plan assets regardless of whether it's a debit or credit difference. When it has a debit balance it is reported as an asset; a credit balance is reported as a liability.

PART D – REPORTING ISSUES

Minimum Pension Liability

The FASB concluded that the prepaid (accrued) pension cost account is insufficient in representing the pension plan when the employer's obligation is underfunded (assets less than liability). So, in that case, any balance in that account should be increased to reflect a minimum liability equal to the underfunded amount. To measure the underfunded liability, we compare the accumulated benefit obligation (ABO) (rather than the PBO) with plan assets. An employer must report a pension liability at least equal to the amount by which its ABO exceeds its plan assets.

Illustration

In our earlier illustration, GT&T Cellular had a PBO of $128 million and plan assets of $104 million at the end of 2003. Suppose, the obligation measured by the accumulated benefits approach (i.e., the ABO) was $110 million. Also suppose that after recording pension expense for 2003 as shown above, the credit balance in the prepaid (accrued) pension cost account was $31 million.

Because the ABO exceeds the plan assets, the minimum liability that must be reported is:

ABO	$110
Plan assets	(104)
Minimum liability	$ 6

In this case, the minimum liability requirement already is satisfied by the prepaid (accrued) pension cost account. Remember, a credit balance in that account is reported as a liability. Therefore, the $31 million liability balance would satisfy the minimum liability requirement. No additional liability would be necessary.

On the other hand, suppose the ABO had exceeded plan assets by $46 million rather than $6 million. In that case, an additional liability of $15 million ($46 million - $31 million) would be needed to satisfy the minimum liability requirement:

	($ in millions)
Intangible pension asset...	15
Additional liability	15

The debit to an intangible asset represents the expectation of future economic benefits from incurring the pension obligation.

Pension Disclosures

Pension amounts reported in the disclosure notes fills a reporting gap left by the amounts reported (or not reported) in the primary financial statements. Disclosures include:

1. A breakdown of the components of the annual pension expense.

2. An estimate of the projected benefit obligation (as well as the accumulated benefit obligation, and vested benefit obligation.

3. Other information to make it possible for interested analysts to reconstruct the financial statements with pension assets and liabilities included.

SELF-STUDY QUESTIONS AND EXERCISES

Concept Review

1. _____ are arrangements designed to provide income to individuals during their retirement years.

2. Funds are set aside in a pension plan during an employee's working years so that the accumulated funds plus _____ are available to replace wages at retirement.

3. A _____ pension plan gains important tax advantages. The employer is permitted an immediate tax deduction for amounts paid into the pension fund. Conversely, the benefits to employees are not taxed until retirement benefits are received.

4. For a pension plan to be qualified for special tax treatment, certain requirements must be met. One is that it must cover at least _____ % of employees.

5. When employees make contributions to a pension plan in addition to employer contributions, it's called a _____ plan.

6. A _____ pension plan promises fixed annual contributions to a pension fund, without further commitment regarding benefit amounts at retirement.

7. The _____ obligation is the pension benefit obligation that is *not* contingent upon an employee's continuing service.

8. The _____ obligation is the discounted present value of retirement benefits calculated by applying the pension formula with no attempt to forecast what salaries will be when the formula actually is applied.

9. The _____ obligation is the present value of those benefits when the actuary includes projected salaries in the pension formula.

10. The projected benefit obligation can change due to periodic _____ cost, accrued _____ , revised _____ , plan _____ , and the payment of _____ .

11. The balance of _____ can change due to investment returns, employer contributions, and the payment of benefits.

12. The _____ reported on the income statement is a composite of periodic changes that occur in both the pension obligation and the plan assets.

13. The _____ in connection with a pension plan is the present value of benefits attributed by the pension formula to employee service during the period, projecting future salary levels (i.e., the projected benefits approach).

14. The _____ is the projected benefit obligation outstanding at the beginning of the period multiplied by the actuary's interest (discount) rate.

15. The _____ return is adjusted for any difference between it and the _____ return before being deducted as a component of pension expense.

16. _____ is the obligation (present value of benefits) due to giving credit to employees for years of service provided before either the date of an amendment to (or initiation of) a pension plan.

17. The _____ method allocates an equal amount of the prior _____ cost to each year.

18. Gains or losses should be deferred until total net gains or losses exceed a defined threshold. Specifically, a *portion* of the excess is included in pension expense only if it exceeds an amount equal to 10% of the _____ , or 10% of _____ , whichever is higher.

Pensions

19. The three components of pension expense that may reduce pension expense are the _____ (always), the amortization of a net _____ , and the amortization of a transition _____ .
20. The components of pension expense that involve delayed recognition are the _____ and the _____ .
21. The difference between the pension expense and the cash contribution is debited or credited, depending on the situation, to a single account: _____ .
22. The difference between the funded status and the balance in prepaid (accrued) pension cost can be reconciled by the unrecognized _____ and the unrecognized _____ . This reconciliation must be disclosed in the financial statements.
23. A minimum liability must be reported to the extent that the _____ exceeds the fair value of _____ .

Answers:
1. Pension plans **2.** earnings from investing those funds **3.** qualified **4.** 70 **5.** contributory
6. defined contribution **7.** vested benefit **8.** accumulated benefit **9.** projected benefit
10. service, interest, estimates, amendments, benefits **11.** plan assets **12.** pension expense
13. service cost **14.** interest cost **15.** actual, expected **16.** Prior service cost **17.** straight-line, service
18. PBO, plan assets **19.** return on plan assets, gain, asset **20.** prior service cost, gains and losses **21.** prepaid (accrued) pension cost **22.** prior service cost, net loss **23.** accumulated benefit obligation, plan assets

REVIEW EXERCISES

Exercise 1

Los Angeles Transport has a noncontributory, defined benefit pension plan. On December 31, 2003 (the end of the company's fiscal period), the following pension-related data were available:

	($ in millions)
Projected benefit obligation:	
Balance, January 1, 2003	$ 600
Service cost	123
Interest cost, *discount rate, 10%*	60
Losses (gains) due to changes in actuarial assumptions in 2003	0
Pension benefits paid	(63)
Balance, December 31, 2003	$ 720
Plan assets:	
Balance, January 1, 2003	$ 450
Actual return on plan assets	45
(Expected return on plan assets, $40)	
Contributions	150
Pension benefits paid	(63)
Balance, December 31, 2003	$ 582
Accumulated benefits obligation, Dec. 31, 2003	$ 630
January 1, 2003, balances:	
Prepaid (accrued) pension cost (credit balance)	$ (8)
Unrecognized prior service cost (amortization $12 per year)	72
Unrecognized net loss (any amortization over 10 years)	70
Intangible pension asset	none

Required:

a. Prepare the 2003 journal entry to record pension expense and funding.

Pensions

b. Prepare the 2003 journal entry to record any necessary additional pension liability. **Show calculations**.

Solution:

a.   ($ in millions)

Pension expense (calculated below)	156*
Prepaid (accrued) pension cost (difference)	6
Cash (given)	150

* Service cost	$123
Interest cost	60
Actual return on the plan assets ($45)	
Adjusted for: $5 gain on the plan assets	(40)
Amortization of prior service cost	12
Amortization of net loss (calculated below)	1
Pension expense	$156

Computation of net loss amortization:

Net loss (previous losses exceeded previous gains)	$70
10% of $600 (greater than $450)	(60)
Amount to be amortized	$10
	÷ 10
Amortization	$ 1

b.   ($ in millions)

Intangible pension asset	34*
Additional liability (calculated below)	34

* The entire $34 million can be added to the intangible asset because its balance will not exceed the unrecognized prior service cost ($72 million - 12 million = $60 million)

Computation of additional liability:

ABO	$(630)
Plan assets	582
Minimum liability	$ (48)
Less: accrued pension cost ($8 + 6)	(14)
Additional liability needed	$ (34)

Exercise 2

The Altar Icon Company sponsors a defined benefit pension plan. The following information pertains to that plan:

Projected benefit obligation at Jan. 1, 2003	$430 million
Service cost for 2003	108 million
Retiree benefits paid during 2003	90 million
Actual and expected return on plan assets for 2003	15 million
Discount rate 10%	

There were no changes in actuarial estimates during 2003.

Required:

Determine Aztar's projected benefit obligation at December 31, 2003.

Solution:

	($ in millions)
Projected benefit obligation at Jan. 1, 2003	$430
Service cost	108
Interest cost (10% x $430)	43
Retiree benefits paid during 2003	(90)
Projected benefit obligation at Dec. 31, 2003	$491

Pensions

Exercise 3

Caraway Service Corporation sponsors a defined benefit pension plan. The following information pertains to that plan:

Projected benefit obligation at Jan. 1, 2003	$5,000 million
Service cost for 2003	960 million
Actual and expected return on plan assets for 2003	210 million
2003 amortization of unrecognized prior service cost	30 million
Retiree benefits paid during 2003	60 million
Discount rate 6%	

Required:

Determine pension expense that Caraway should report in its 2003 income statement.

Solution:

	($ in millions)
Service cost	$960
Interest cost (6% x $5,000)	300
Return on plan assets	(210)
Amortization of prior service cost	30
Pension expense	$1,080

MULTIPLE CHOICE

Enter the letter corresponding to the response that **best** completes each of the following statements or questions.

_____ 1. In an employer-sponsored defined benefit pension plan, the interest cost included in the pension expense represents:
a. The effective discount rate times the unamortized balance of prior service costs.
b. The increase in the projected benefit obligation due to the passage of time.
c. The increase in the fair value of plan assets due to the passage of time.
d. The difference between the actual and expected returns on plan assets.

_____ 2. Van Nuen Inc. began a defined-benefit pension plan for its employees on January 1, 2003. The following data are provided for 2003, as of December 31, 2003:

Projected benefit obligation	$785,000
Accumulated benefit obligation	740,000
Plan assets at fair value	655,000
Pension expense	715,000
Employer's cash contribution (end of year)	655,000

What amount should Van Nuen record as additional minimum pension liability at December 31, 2003?
a. $85,000
b. $60,000
c. $25,000
d. $0

_____ 3. Dividends from stock investments by a pension plan are reported by the employer as:
a. Investment revenue on an accrual basis.
b. Investment revenue on a cash basis.
c. A reduction of the periodic pension expense.
d. A reduction of the projected benefit obligation (PBO).

_____ 4. The component of periodic pension expense that represents the actuarial present value of the increase in an employer's pension obligation to employees because of their services rendered during the current period is the:
a. Current cost.
b. Service cost.
c. Accumulated benefit obligation (ABO).
d. Projected benefit obligation (PBO).

Pensions

____ 5. The Colorado Copper Company sponsors a defined benefit pension plan. The following information pertains to that plan:

Projected benefit obligation at Jan. 1, 2003	$144 million
Service cost for 2003	36 million
Retiree benefits paid (end of year)	30 million
Discount rate	10%

No change in actuarial estimates occurred during 2003. What is CCC's projected benefit obligation at December 31, 2003?
a. $164.4 million
b. $158.4 million
c. $150.0 million
d. $128.4 million

____ 6. Panther Products sponsors a defined benefit pension plan. The following information pertains to that plan:

Service cost for 2003	$480 million
Actual and expected return on plan assets for 2003	105 million
2000 amortization of unrecognized prior service cost	15 million
Interest on pension obligation for 2003	150 million
Retiree benefits paid during 2003	30 million

The pension expense that Panther should report in its 2003 income statement is:
a. $510 million
b. $540 million
c. $630 million
d. $750 million

____ 7. Information regarding the defined-benefit pension plan of Pauline Products included the following for 2003 ($ in millions):

January 1:	
Accrued pension cost	$ 2
December 31:	
Projected benefit obligation (PBO)	$85
Accumulated benefit obligation (ABO)	75
Plan assets	50
Pension expense	8

No contributions were made to the pension plan assets during 2003. At December 31, 2003, what amount should Hall record as additional pension liability?
a. $15 million
b. $23 million
c. $25 million
d. $32 million

Intermediate Accounting, 3/e

_____ 8. Information regarding the defined-benefit pension plan of Amber Beverages included the following for 2003 ($ in millions):

Prepaid pension cost, January 1 (debit balance)	$ 20
Service cost	490
Interest cost	380
Actual and expected return on plan assets	220
Amortization of unrecognized net loss	30
Prior service cost	none
Employer contributions to the pension plan (end of year)	500

The accumulated benefit obligation was less than the fair value of plan assets at December 31, 2003. Amber should report accrued pension cost at December 31, 2003, in the amount of:
a. $140 million
b. $160 million
c. $200 million
d. $640 million

_____ 9. Information regarding the defined-benefit pension plan of Tri Cities Transport included the following for 2003 ($ in millions):

Service cost	$48
Interest cost	32
Actual and expected return on plan assets	26
Amortization of unrecognized net gain	3
Amortization of unrecognized prior service cost	5
Retiree benefits paid (end of year)	50

What is Tri Cities' pension expense for 2003?
a. $56 million
b. $62 million
c. $98 million
d. $164 million

_____ 10. Information regarding the defined-benefit pension plan of Certainty Services included the following for 2003 ($ in millions):

Plan assets, January 1	$ 70
Plan assets, December 31	105
Retiree benefits paid (end of year)	17
Employer contributions to the pension plan (end of year)	42

What amount should Certainty use as the actual return on plan assets when computing pension expense for 2003?
a. $10 million
b. $24 million
c. $35 million
d. $60 million

____ 11. Information regarding the defined-benefit pension plan of Neo Products included the following for 2003 ($ in millions):

Plan assets, January 1	$210
Plan assets, December 31	315
Return on plan assets	30
Employer contributions to the pension plan (end of year)	126

What amount of retiree benefits was paid at the end of 2003?
a. $21 million
b. $51 million
c. $72 million
d. $105 million

____ 12. Information regarding the defined-benefit pension plan of Melrose Products included the following for 2003 ($ in millions):

Plan assets, January 1	$350
Plan assets, December 31	525
Retiree benefits paid (end of year)	85
Return on plan assets	50

What were the employer contributions to the pension plan at the end of 2003?
a. $30 million
b. $175 million
c. $210 million
d. $225 million

____ 13. Information regarding the defined-benefit pension plan of Glavin Industries included the following for 2003 ($ in millions):

Plan assets, January 1	$210
Retiree benefits paid (end of year)	150
Actual return on plan assets	30
Employer contributions to the pension plan (end of year)	126
Expected rate of return on plan assets	10%

What amount should Glavin report in its disclosure notes for plan assets at December 31, 2003?
a. $156 million
b. $207 million
c. $216 million
d. $516 million

_____ 14. Information regarding the defined-benefit pension plan of Regional Health Services included the following for 2003 ($ in millions):

Prepaid pension cost, January 1 (debit balance)	$ 15
Service cost	240
Interest cost	170
Actual and expected return on plan assets	150
Amortization of unrecognized net gain	20
Prior service cost	none
Employer contributions to the pension plan (end of year)	200

The accumulated benefit obligation was less than the fair value of plan assets at December 31, 2003. What should Regional report in its balance sheet at December 31, 2003, for prepaid (accrued) pension cost?
a. $25 million liability
b. $95 million liability
c. $395 million liability
d. $15 million asset and $80 million liability

_____ 15. In the disclosure notes that accompany its financial statements a company with a defined benefit pension plan must report a reconciliation of the:
a. Vested benefit obligation with the accumulated benefit obligation.
b. Pension expense reported in the income statement with the prepaid (accrued) pension cost reported in the balance sheet.
c. Accumulated benefit obligation with the projected benefit obligation.
d. Prepaid (accrued) pension cost with the funded status of the plan.

Answers:

1.	b.	6.	b.	11.	b.
2.	c.	7.	a.	12.	c.
3.	c.	8.	b.	13.	c.
4.	b.	9.	a.	14.	a.
5.	a.	10.	a.	15.	d.

Employee Benefit Plans

LEARNING OBJECTIVES

After studying this chapter, you should be able to:

1. Describe the nature of postretirement benefit plans other than pensions and identify the similarities and differences in accounting for those plans and pensions.
2. Explain how the obligation for postretirement benefits is measured and how the obligation changes.
3. Determine the components of postretirement benefit expense.
4. Explain and implement the elective fair value approach for stock compensation plans.
5. Explain and implement the alternate intrinsic value approach to accounting for stock compensation plans.
6. Explain and implement the accounting for stock appreciation rights and differentiate between those that create liabilities and those that create equity.
7. Identify other preretirement compensation plans and the accounting treatment of those plans.

CHAPTER HIGHLIGHTS

PART A: POSTRETIREMENT BENEFITS OTHER THAN PENSIONS

Postretirement benefits include a variety of retiree health and welfare benefits other than pensions. Benefits can include medical coverage, dental coverage, life insurance, group legal services, and other benefits. The largest and most common of these is health care benefits. Eligibility usually is based on age and/or years of service.

To the extent possible, we account for postretirement benefits the same way as pension benefits. Any accounting differences are due to fundamental differences between pensions and other postretirement benefits. However, there are more similarities than differences. Like pensions, other postretirement benefits are a form of deferred compensation. From an accounting perspective, the main difference is that the amount of *postretirement health care* benefits typically is unrelated to service. Instead, it's usually an "all-or-nothing" plan in which a certain level of coverage is promised upon retirement, and the coverage is independent of the length of service beyond the eligibility date. So, unlike pensions, their cost is "attributed" to the years from the employee's date of hire to the "full eligibility date."

The Postretirement Benefit Obligation

The company's actuary estimates what the net cost of postretirement benefits will be for current employees (and dependents) in each year of their expected retirement. The discounted present value of those costs is the company's liability. The actuary's estimate of the total postretirement benefits (at their discounted present value) expected to be received by plan participants is the Expected Postretirement Benefit Obligation (EPBO). The portion of the EPBO attributed to employee service to date is the Accumulated Postretirement Benefit Obligation (APBO).

Illustration

The actuary for Brahms Banisters estimates the net cost of providing health care benefits to retired employees during their retirement years to have a present value of $80 million as of the end of 2003. This is the EPBO. Suppose the benefits and therefore the costs relate to an average 40 years of service and that on average 8 of those years have been completed.

The APBO would be:

$$\underset{\text{EPBO}}{\$80 \text{ million}} \quad \times \quad \underset{\substack{\text{fraction attributed} \\ \text{to service to date}}}{^{8}/_{40}} \quad = \quad \underset{\text{APBO}}{\$16 \text{ million}}$$

A year later, the EPBO might have changed because of changes in some of the assumptions used to calculate it and because of a year's interest accruing at the discount rate, but not because of service. This is because, unlike in pension plans, the *total* obligation is not increased by an additional year's service. It is an estimate of the total cost of providing benefits to employees who are expected to eventually become eligible.

The service cost, then, is due to *attributing* $^{9}/_{40}$ of the EPBO a year later to service performed to date rather than $^{8}/_{40}$. The cost of benefits is attributed to the years during which employees are expected to become fully eligible for the benefits. This means assigning an equal fraction ($^{1}/_{40}$ in our illustration) of the EPBO to each year of service from the employee's date of hire to the employee's "full eligibility date." The full eligibility date is the date the employee has performed all the service necessary to have earned all the retiree benefits estimated to be received by that employee. The attribution period does not include years of service beyond the full eligibility date even when employees are expected to work after that date because at the full eligibility date employees have earned the right to receive the full benefits expected under the plan, and the amount of the benefits will not increase with service beyond that date.

The interest cost is the discount rate times the APBO at the beginning of the year.

The APBO can change for the following reasons:

APBO at the *beginning* of the year

* ▶ **Plus: Prior service cost** - Cost of making amendments retroactive to prior years
* ▶ **Plus: Service cost** - Portion of the EPBO attributed to the current period
* ▶ **Plus: Interest cost** - Accrual of interest as time passes (beg. APBO x discount rate)
* ▶ **Plus (minus): Loss (gain) on APBO** - Adjustments to APBO when estimates change
* ▶ <u>**Less: Retiree benefits paid** - Benefits actually paid to retired employees</u>

APBO at the *end* of the year

The Plan Assets

Unlike pension plans, many postretirement benefit plans are not funded, meaning no plan assets are specifically set aside to pay benefits when they come due. Plans that are funded often are significantly underfunded. However, when postretirement benefit plans are funded, the plan assets change for the same reasons they do with pension plans. The trustee reports to the employer the changes in assets of a postretirement benefit fund, which include the following:

Plan assets at the *beginning* of the year

* ▶ **Plus: Return on plan assets** - Dividends, interest, market price appreciation
* ▶ **Plus: Cash contributions** - Employer contributions
* ▶ <u>**Less: Retiree benefits paid** - Benefits actually paid to retired employees</u>

Plan assets at the *end* of the year

Postretirement Benefit Expense

The components of postretirement benefit expense are essentially the same as those for pension expense. The periodic expense is a composite of periodic changes in both the APBO and the plan assets (if any). Specifically, postretirement benefit expense includes:

* **Service cost** - Increase in the APBO attributed to employee service this year
* **Interest cost** - Accrual of interest as time passes (beg. APBO x discount rate)
* **Actual return on the plan assets** - Dividends, interest, price appreciation
    Adjusted for: Loss or gain - difference between actual and expected return
* **Amortization of prior service cost**
* **Amortization of the net loss or net gain**
* <u>**Amortization of the transition liability** - APBO when SFAS 106 was first implemented</u>
    Postretirement benefit expense

The transition obligation could be expensed either immediately or on a straight-line basis over the plan participants' future service periods (optionally over a 20-year period if that's longer). Most companies chose to recognize the entire transition obligation immediately upon adopting SFAS 106 in 1994, and thus would not have the sixth component of postretirement benefit expense.

Illustration

Actuary and trustee reports indicate the following changes in the APBO and plan assets of GT&T Cellular during 2003:

Prior service cost from plan amendment at the beginning of 2003	$52 million
Unrecognized net gain at Jan.1, 2003 (previous gains exceeded previous losses)	$50 million
Average remaining period to full eligibility for the active employee group	13 years
Actuary's discount rate	5%

($ in millions)

	APBO			PLAN ASSETS
Beginning of 2003	$240	*Beginning* of 2003		$200
Service cost	26	Return on plan assets,		
Interest cost, 5%	12	5% (7% expected)		10
Loss (gain) on PBO	(2)	Cash contributions		18
Less: Retiree benefits	(20)	Less: Retiree benefits		(20)
End of 2000	$256	*End* of 2000		$208

Calculation of pension expense:

($ in millions)

Service cost (from APBO above)		$26
Interest cost (from APBO above)		12
Actual return on the plan assets (from Plan Assets above)	$10	
Adjusted for: loss on the plan assets ([7%-5%] x $200)	4	
Expected return on the plan assets		(14)
Amortization of prior service cost ($52 ÷ 13 years)		4
Amortization of the net gain*		(2)
Postretirement benefit expense		$26

* Amortization of the net gain:

($ in millions)

Net gain (previous gains exceeded previous losses)	$50
10% of $240 ($240 is greater than $200): the "corridor"	24
Excess at the beginning of the year	$26
Average remaining service period	÷ 13 years
Amount amortized to 2003 postretirement benefit expense	$ 2

PART B: STOCK-BASED COMPENSATION PLANS

Many compensation plans include one or more types of stock-based awards. These include outright awards of shares, stock options, or cash payments tied to the market price of shares. Usually, an executive compensation plan is tied to performance in a way that uses compensation to motivate its recipients.

Regardless of the form such a plan takes, the accounting objective is to record compensation expense over the periods in which related services are performed. That means we need to (a) determine the value of the compensation and (b) expense that compensation over the periods in which participants perform services.

Stock Award Plans

Sometimes the compensation is a grant of shares of stock. In that case, the shares usually are restricted in a way that benefits are tied to continued employment. Shares usually are subject to forfeiture by the employee if employment is terminated within some specified number of years from the date of grant and the employee cannot sell the shares during the restriction period.

The compensation is the market price of unrestricted shares of the same stock and is accrued as compensation expense over the service period for which participants receive the shares. This usually is the period from the date of grant to when restrictions are lifted (the vesting date).

Illustration

Under its restricted stock award plan, Ford Storage grants 6 million of its $1 par common shares to division managers at January 1, 2003. The shares are subject to forfeiture if managers leave the company within three years. Shares have a current market price of $15 per share.

Total compensation:

$15	fair value per share
x 6 million	shares awarded
= $90 million	total compensation

The total compensation is to be allocated to expense over the 3-year service (vesting) period: 2003 - 2005

$90 million ÷ 3 years = $30 million per year

	($ in millions)
December 31, 2003, 2004, 2005	
Compensation expense ($90 million ÷ 3 years)..	30
Paid-in capital – restricted stock	30
December 31, 2005	
Paid-in capital – restricted stock (6 million shares at $15)	90
Common stock (6 million shares at $1 par)...	6
Paid-in capital – excess of par (to balance)	84

Employee Benefit Plans

If restricted stock is forfeited because, say, the employee quits the company, related entries previously made would simply be reversed.

Stock Option Plans

Stock option plans give recipients the option to purchase (a) a specified number of shares of the firm's stock, (b) at a specified price, (c) during a specified period of time. Although the accounting objective is to report compensation expense during the period of service for which the compensation is given, a heated issue is how to measure the value of stock options.

Elective fair value approach. After long debate, the FASB decided to encourage, rather than require, that the fair value of options be recognized as expense. By the elective fair value approach, compensation is measured at the grant date using an option-pricing model that considers the exercise price and expected term of the option, the current market price of the underlying stock and its expected volatility, expected dividends, and the expected risk-free rate of return.

Illustration

Under its executive stock option plan, Ford Storage grants options at January 1, 2003, that permit division managers to acquire 6 million of the company's $1 par common shares within the next 7 years, but not before December 31, 2005 (the vesting date). The exercise price is the market price of the shares on the date of grant, $15 per share. The fair value of the options, estimated by an appropriate option pricing model, is $5 per option.

Total compensation:

$5	estimated fair value per option
x 6 million	options granted
= $30 million	total compensation

The total compensation is to be allocated to expense over the 3-year service (vesting) period: 2003 - 2005

$30 million ÷ 3 years = $10 million per year

December 31, 2003, 2004, 2005	($ in millions)
Compensation expense ($30 million ÷ 3 years)...	10
Paid-in capital – stock options..	10

Alternate intrinsic value approach. Most companies choose *not* to adopt the elective fair value approach and continue to account for options in accordance with APB Opinion 25 issued in 1972. By the alternate intrinsic value approach, the value of fixed options is measured at the grant date in an amount equal to their "intrinsic values" rather than their fair values. Intrinsic value is simply the difference between the market price of the shares and the exercise price at which they can be acquired (the benefit the holder of an option would realize by exercising the option and immediately selling the underlying stock). An option that permits an employee to buy $15 stock for $12 has an intrinsic value of $3. Compensation is measured as the "intrinsic value" of the award and expensed over the service period, usually from the date of grant to the vesting date.

An option whose exercise price equals the market price of the underlying stock has zero intrinsic value and *no compensation* is recorded for the options. The exercise price of most options is the market price at the date of grant. So, most options result in zero compensation expense for the granting companies.

Stock Appreciation Rights (SARs)

Unlike stock options, SARs enable an employee to benefit by the amount that the market price of the company's stock rises, but without having to buy shares. At exercise, the employee receives the "share appreciation" since the date of grant. This is the increase in the market price over a prespecified price (usually the market price at the date of grant). Thus, if the market price has risen from $15 to, say, $25, the employee receives $10 cash for each SAR held. Usually, the share appreciation is payable in cash but may be payable in shares equal in value to the share appreciation.

From an accounting perspective, the award is considered to be equity if the employer can elect to settle in shares of stock rather than cash. However, if the employee can elect to receive cash (which usually is the case), the award is considered to be a liability. Either way, the amount of compensation must be continually adjusted to reflect changes in the market price of stock until the compensation is finally paid unless the award is considered equity and the elective fair value approach is used. In that case, fair value is measured at the grant date.

Illustration

Ford Storage grants 6 million SARs to key managers at January 1, 2003. The SARs permit managers to receive cash equal to the excess of the market price at exercise over the share price at the date of grant ($15). The SARs vest at the end of 2005 (cannot be exercised until then) and expire at the end of 2007.

December 31, 2003 (Market price $18) ($ in millions)

Compensation expense* 6

    Liability – SAR plan 6

* Calculation:

$$[\$18\text{-}15] \times 6 \text{ million} \quad \times \quad \tfrac{1}{3} \quad - \quad \$0 \quad = \quad \$6$$

estimated total compensation	fraction of service to date	expensed earlier	current expense

December 31, 2004 (Market price $17) ($ in millions)

Compensation expense* 2

    Liability – SAR plan 2

* Calculation:

$$[\$17\text{-}15] \times 6 \text{ million} \quad \times \quad \tfrac{2}{3} \quad - \quad \$6 \quad = \quad \$2$$

estimated total compensation	fraction of service to date	expensed earlier	current expense

December 31, 2005 (Market price $17)   ($ in millions)

Compensation expense* 4

    Liability – SAR plan 4

* Calculation:

$$[\$17\text{-}15] \times 6 \text{ million} \qquad \times \qquad {}^{3}\!/_{3} \qquad - \qquad \$8 \qquad = \qquad \$4$$

estimated total compensation		fraction of service to date		expensed earlier		current expense

Compensation expense and the liability are adjusted the same way each period until the SARs expire or are exercised.

PART C: OTHER COMPENSATION PRIOR TO RETIREMENT

Other preretirement compensation plans include annual bonuses, performance share plans, long-term cash bonuses, performance unit plans, and phantom stock plans. Regardless of the name and specific form of the plan, the accounting objective is to record compensation over the appropriate service period.

Compensation for Future Absences

An employer accrues an expense and related liability for employees' compensation for future absences such as vacation pay if the obligation meets four conditions:

1. The obligation is attributable to employees' services already performed.
2. The paid absence can be taken in a later year – the benefit vests (will be compensated even if employment is terminated) or the benefit can be accumulated over time.
3. Payment is probable.
4. The amount can be reasonably estimated.

Postemployment Benefits

Employers often provide benefits to former or inactive employees after employment but before retirement. "Postemployment" (rather than "postretirement") benefits sometimes include salary continuation, severance benefits, supplemental unemployment benefits, disability-related benefits, job training and counseling, and continuation of benefits such as health care benefits and life insurance coverage.

Sometimes "post-employment" benefits meet the criteria for accrual as compensated absences and should be accounted for as compensation for future absences. If the conditions above are met the liability should be accrued. Otherwise, "post-employment" benefits should be treated as loss contingencies.

SELF-STUDY QUESTIONS AND EXERCISES

Concept Review

1. Sometimes a company's consistent practice of providing postretirement benefits a certain way is a better indication of the employer's real plan for benefits than the written plan. In those cases, the _____ plan should override the written plan in determining the basis for accounting for postretirement benefits.

2. The _____ postretirement benefit obligation is the actuary's estimate of the total postretirement benefits (at their discounted present value) expected to be received by plan participants.

3. The _____ postretirement benefit obligation measures the obligation existing at a particular date, rather than the total amount expected to be earned by plan participants.

4. The APBO is conceptually similar to a pension plan's _____ benefit obligation.

5. The cost of benefits is _____ to the years during which those benefits are assumed to be earned by employees.

6. The attribution period spans each year of service from the employee's date of hire to the employee's _____ date, which is the date the employee has performed all the service necessary to have earned all the retiree benefits estimated to be received by that employee.

7. The _____ obligation could be recognized as part of the compensation expense by either of two methods. An employer could choose to recognize the entire amount immediately as the cumulative effect of a change in accounting principle, or on a straight-line basis over the plan participants' future service periods (or optionally over a ___-year period if that's longer.)

8. The _____ cost for retiree health care plans is an allocation to the current year of a portion of the EPBO.

9. _____ shares usually are subject to forfeiture by the employee if employment is terminated between the date of grant and a specified vesting date.

10. The fair value of shares awarded under a restricted stock award plan is accrued to compensation expense over the service period for which participants receive the shares. This usually is the period from the date of grant to the _____ date.

11. The _____ of a stock option is determined by employing a recognized option pricing model.

12. An option pricing model should take into account the (1) _____ price of the option, (2) expected _____ of the option, (3) _____ price of the stock, (4) expected dividends, (5) expected _____ rate of return during the term of the option, and (6) expected _____ of the stock.

13. The recipient pays no tax at the time of the grant or the exercise of the options under an _____ plan. Instead, the tax on the difference between the option price and the market price at the exercise date is paid on the date any shares acquired are subsequently sold. The employer gets no tax deduction at all.

14. The employee cannot delay paying tax under a _____ plan.

15. By the traditional alternative approach for accounting for stock options, compensation is recorded only when options have _____ value.

16. Under the FASB elective approach, compensation would be accrued in the amount of the _____ value of the options at the grant date.

17. The fair value of stock options has two essential components:
   (1) _____ value and (2) _____ value.

18. An option that allows an employee to buy $25 stock for $14 has an intrinsic value of $ _____.

19. The accounting treatment of SARs depends on whether the award is considered an equity instrument or a liability. If the employer can choose to settle in shares rather than cash, the award is considered to be _____ . If the employee will receive cash or can choose to receive cash, the award is considered to be a _____ .

20. The accounting treatment of any of the various bonus plans is to accrue _____ and a related _____ annually based on the estimated eventual value of compensation.

21. An employer should accrue an expense and the related liability for employees' compensation for future absences, like vacation pay, if the obligation meets each of four conditions: (1) the obligation is attributable to employees' services _____ , (2) the paid absence can be taken in a later year, (3) the payment is _____ , (4) the amount can be reasonably _____ .

22. If "postemployment" benefits meet the criteria for accrual as compensated absences. a company should recognize the obligation to provide these benefits (debit expense; credit liability). Otherwise, postemployment benefits should be treated as _____ and accrued when it is probable that a liability has been incurred and the amount can be reasonably estimated.

Answers:
1. substantive **2.** expected **3.** accumulated **4.** projected **5.** attributed **6.** full eligibility
7. transition 20 **8.** service **9.** Restricted **10.** vesting **11.** fair value **12.** exercise, term, current market, risk-free, volatility **13.** incentive **14.** nonqualified **15.** intrinsic **16.** fair
17. intrinsic, time **18.** 11 **19.** equity, liability **20.** compensation expense, liability **21.** already performed, probable, estimated **22.** loss contingencies

REVIEW EXERCISES

Exercise 1

Chicago Products has a postretirement benefit plan that provides health care benefits to retirees. The company adopted *SFAS 106* for the 1994 fiscal year. The APBO at that date was $750 million and the plan was not funded, resulting in a transition obligation of $750 million at the beginning of the year. The transition obligation was to be amortized over the 15-year average remaining service period of plan participants active at the beginning of the year. Chicago Products began funding at the end of 1994. Pertinent data were as follows:

Discount rate	8 %
Expected rate of return on plan assets	10 %
1994 service cost	$ 48 million
Employer contribution to plan assets (end of year)	110 million
Retiree benefit payments (end of year)	40 million

Because of changes in assumptions and estimates of health care costs at the end of 1994, the APBO was determined to be $94 million higher than anticipated.

Required:

1. Determine the accumulated postretirement benefit obligation (APBO) at the **end** of fiscal year 1994.

2. Determine postretirement benefit expense for fiscal year 1994.

3. Prepare the journal entry to record postretirement benefit expense and funding for fiscal year 1994.

4. Prepare a schedule to reconcile the funded status of the plan with the amount reported on the balance sheet for fiscal year 1994.

Solution:

Requirement 1

	($ in millions)
APBO:	
Beginning	$750
Service cost	48
Interest cost (8% x $750)	60
Loss on APBO	94
Benefit payments	(40)
Ending	$912

Requirement 2

Service cost	$ 48
Interest cost	60
Amortization of transition obligation ($750/15)	50
Postretirement benefit expense	$158

Requirement 3

Postretirement benefit expense (determined above)	158	
Accrued postretirement benefit cost (difference)...		48
Cash (given)..		110

Requirement 4

APBO	$(912)
Plan assets ($110 - 40)	70
Funded status	$(842)
Unrecognized net loss	94
Unrecognized transition obligation ($750 - 50)	700
Accrued postretirement benefit cost	$ (48)

Exercise 2

New York Laminating Corporation provides a variety of stock-based compensation plans to its employees. Under its executive stock option plan, the company granted options on January 1, 2003, that permit executives to acquire 6 million of the company's $1 par common shares within the next 7 years, but not before December 31, 2005 (the vesting date). The exercise price is the market price of the shares on the date of grant, $15.50 per share. The fair value of the 6 million options, estimated by an appropriate option-pricing model, is $4 per option. No forfeitures are anticipated. Ignore taxes.

Required:
1. Determine the total compensation cost pertaining to the options, assuming New York chooses to follow the FASB's elective accounting approach for fixed compensation plans.

2. Prepare the appropriate journal entry (if any) to record the award of options on January 1, 2003.

3. Prepare the appropriate journal entry (if any) to record compensation expense on December 31, 2003.

Employee Benefit Plans

Solution:

Requirement 1

$4	fair value per option
x 6 million	options granted
= $24 million	fair value of award

Requirement 2

no entry

Requirement 3

($ in millions)

Compensation expense ($24 million ÷ 3 years)   8
    Paid-in capital - stock options..   8

Exercise 3

Bennett Plastics has 20 employees. Each employee is granted 2 weeks of paid vacation per year. Vacation time not taken in the year earned can be carried over to subsequent years. At the end of 2003, four employees, each of who earn $800 per week, had vacation time carryovers as follows:

Employee	Vacation Weeks Earned	Vacation Time Taken
Laverne	2	1
Shirley	2	0
Ren	2	0
Stimpy	2	1

Required:

1. Calculate the amount of any **liability** that Bennett should accrue at Dec. 31, 2003, for vacation time.

2. Prepare the **journal entry** to record vacation salaries.

```
Solution:
Requirement 1

    Weeks earned                        8
    Time taken                        (2)
    Untaken vacation time               6
                                    x $800
    Liability for vacation time      $4,800

Requirement 2

    Salaries expense ..........................................................    4,800
        Liability - compensated absences ...........................................         4,800
```

MULTIPLE CHOICE

Enter the letter corresponding to the response that **best** completes each of the following statements or questions.

____ 1. On January 1, 2003, DeSoto Industries' accumulated postretirement benefit obligation was $75 million. Retiree benefits of $9 million were paid at the end of 2003. Service cost for 2003 is $21 million.

Estimates and assumptions regarding future health care costs were revised in 2003, causing the actuary to revise downward the estimate of the APBO by $2 million. The actuary's discount rate is 8%. There were no unrecognized postretirement benefit costs at the end of 2003.

What is the accumulated postretirement benefit obligation at December 31, 2003?
a. $ 91 million
b. $ 93 million
c. $100 million
d. $102 million

____ 2. On December 31, 2003, Staymore Inns' accumulated postretirement benefit obligation was $273 million. Retiree benefits of $27 million were paid at the end of 2003. Service cost for 2003 is $63 million.

Estimates and assumptions regarding future health care costs were revised in 2003, causing the actuary to revise downward the estimate of the APBO by $6 million. The actuary's discount rate is 8%. There were no unrecognized postretirement benefit costs at the end of 2003.

What was the accumulated postretirement benefit obligation at January 1, 2003?
a. $200 million
b. $210 million
c. $225 million
d. $273 million

____ 3. On December 31, 2003, the expected postretirement benefit obligation was $300 million. The accumulated postretirement benefit obligation was $175 million. Service cost for 2004 was $60 million. The actuary's discount rate is 8%. What was the interest cost for 2004?
a. $14.0 million
b. $18.8 million
c. $24.0 million
d. $28.8 million

____ 4. Imagine Publishers, Inc. sponsors a postretirement plan providing health care benefits. The following information relates to the current year's activity of Imagine's postretirement benefit plan:

Service cost	$120 million
Actual and expected return on plan assets	30 million
Interest cost	40 million
Amortization of net loss	10 million
Amortization of prior service cost	5 million
Amortization of transition obligation	15 million
Retiree benefits paid (end of year)	35 million

What is Imagine's postretirement benefit expense?
a. $140 million
b. $150 million
c. $160 million
d. $185 million

_____ 5.   Expansion, Inc. sponsors an unfunded postretirement plan providing health care benefits. The following information relates to the current year's activity of Expansion's postretirement benefit plan:

Service cost	$120 million
Interest cost	40 million
Amortization of net gain	10 million
Prior service cost	none
Transition obligation	none
Retiree benefits paid (end of year)	35 million

What is Expansion's postretirement benefit expense?
a. $115 million
b. $150 million
c. $160 million
d. $170 million

_____ 6.   Starr Builders sponsors an unfunded postretirement plan providing health care benefits. The following information relates to the current year's activity of Starr's postretirement benefit plan:

Service cost	$240 million
Amortization of net gain	20 million
Prior service cost	none
Transition obligation	none
Retiree benefits paid (end of year)	60 million
Postretirement benefit expense	$300 million

What Starr's interest cost for the year?
a. $40 million
b. $80 million
c. $60 million
d. $100 million

_____ 7.   Richmond Products, Inc. sponsors a postretirement plan providing health care benefits to employees who have completed at least 10 years service and are age 53 years or older at retirement. To date, the employees that have retired under the plan have an average age of 60. No employee has worked beyond age 65. Crystal Alicea was hired when she was 46 years old. The attribution period for accruing Richmond's expected postretirement health care benefit obligation to Alicea is during the period when Alicea is:
a.   53 to 60 years old
b.   53 to 65 years old
c.   46 to 56 years old
d.   46 to 65 years old

Items 8 and 9 are based on the following:

On January 1, 2003, Olympic Insurance Company granted 30,000 stock options to certain executives. The options are exercisable no sooner than December 31, 2005, and expire on January 1, 2008. Each option can be exercised to acquire one share of $1 par common stock for $12. An option-pricing model estimates the fair value of the options to be $5 on the date of grant. The market price of Olympic's stock was as follows:

January 1, 2003 $14
December 31, 2003   15

____ 8. If Olympic chooses the FASB's elective accounting approach, what amount should Olympic recognize as compensation expense for 2003?
    a. $10,000
    b. $20,000
    c. $30,000
    d. $50,000

____ 9. If Olympic does **not** choose the FASB's elective accounting approach, what amount should Olympic recognize as compensation expense for 2003?
    a. $10,000
    b. $20,000
    c. $30,000
    d. $50,000

____ 10. On January 1, 2003, Jackson Corporation granted its CEO, 40,000 stock appreciation rights, which are exercisable no sooner than December 31, 2006, and expire on January 1, 2009. On exercise, the CEO will receive cash for the excess of the stock's market price on the exercise date over the market price on the grant date. The market price of Jackson's stock was $20 on January 1, 2003, and $25 on December 31, 2003. As a result of the stock appreciation rights, Jackson Corporation should recognize compensation expense for 2003 of
    a. $0
    b. $ 33,333
    c. $ 50,000
    d. $400,000

___ 11. On January 2, 2003, Wilson, Inc. granted Brice Wilson, its president, 15,000 stock appreciation rights that are exercisable no sooner than December 31, 2005, and expire on January 1, 2008. On exercise, Wilson will receive cash for the excess of the stock's market price on the exercise date over the market price on the grant date. The market price of Wilson's stock was $40 on January 2, 2003, and $50 on December 31, 2003. As a result of the stock appreciation rights, Wilson Inc. should recognize compensation expense for 2003 of
   a. $0
   b. $ 30,000
   c. $ 50,000
   d. $150,000

___ 12. On January 1, 2003, Unified Systems granted its division managers 100,000 stock appreciation rights. The SARs are exercisable no sooner than December 31, 2006, and expire on January 1, 2010. Upon exercise, the division managers can elect to receive cash or common stock equal to the excess of the stock's market price on the exercise date over the market price on the grant date. The market price of Unified's stock was as follows:

January 1, 2003	$30
December 31, 2003	34
December 31, 2004	36

As a result of the stock appreciation rights, Unified should recognize compensation expense for 2004 of:
   a. $0
   b. $100,000
   c. $150,000
   d. $200,000

___ 13. On January 1, 2003, Baddour Nursery Products granted 400,000 stock appreciation rights to certain executives. The SARs are exercisable no sooner than December 31, 2005, and expire on January 1, 2008. Upon exercise, the executives will receive cash equal to the excess of the stock's market price on the exercise date over the market price on the grant date. The market price of Baddour's stock was as follows:

January 1, 2003	$15
December 31, 2003	16
December 31, 2004	18

As a result of the stock appreciation rights, what liability should Baddour recognize in its 2004 balance sheet?
   a. $0
   b. $300,000
   c. $400,000
   d. $800,000

____ 14. On January 1, 2003, Yukon Company agreed to grant its employees two weeks vacation each year, with the provision that vacations earned in a particular year could be taken the following year. For the year ended December 31, 2003, all twelve of Yukon's employees earned $1,200 per week each. Eight of these vacation weeks were not taken during 2003. In Yukon's 2003 income statement, how much expense should be reported for compensated absences?
   a. $0
   b. $9,600
   c. $14,400
   d. $28,800

____ 15. An enterprise should accrue a liability for compensation of employees' unpaid vacations if certain conditions exist. Each of the following is a condition for accrual except:
   a. Compensation for the vacations is probable.
   b. The employee has the right to carry forward the vacation time beyond the current period.
   c. The amount of compensation is known.
   d. The employee benefit has been earned.

Answers:

1.	a.	6.	b.	11.	c.
2.	c.	7.	c.	12.	d.
3.	a.	8.	d.	13.	d.
4.	c.	9.	b.	14.	b.
5.	b.	10.	c.	15.	c.

Shareholders' Equity

LEARNING OBJECTIVES

After studying this chapter, you should be able to:

1. Describe the components of shareholders' equity and explain how they are reported.
2. Prepare a statement of shareholders' equity and explain its usefulness.
3. Record the issuance of shares when sold for cash, noncash consideration, and by share purchase contract.
4. Describe what occurs when shares are retired and how the retirement is recorded.
5. Distinguish between accounting for retired shares and treasury shares.
6. Describe retained earnings and distinguish it from paid-in capital.
7. Explain the basis of corporate dividends, including the similarities and differences between cash and property dividends.
8. Explain stock dividends and stock splits and how they are accounted for.

CHAPTER HIGHLIGHTS

PART A: THE NATURE OF SHAREHOLDERS' EQUITY

Businesses raise money externally to fund operations in two ways – debt financing and equity financing. Debt financing takes the form of notes, bonds, leases, and other liabilities. These create creditors' interest in the assets of the business. Equity financing creates ownership interests in the assets of the business. Owners of a corporation are its shareholders. Shareholders' equity is a residual amount. That is, it's the amount that remains after creditor claims have been subtracted from assets (net assets). Remember, net assets equal shareholders' equity:

$$\underbrace{\text{Assets} - \text{Liabilities}}_{\textit{Net Assets}} = \text{Shareholders' equity}$$

Shareholders' Equity in Financial Statements

Shareholders' equity arises primarily from (a) amounts invested by shareholders and (b) amounts earned by the firm on behalf of its shareholders. These two amounts are reported in two categories on a balance sheet: paid-in capital and retained earnings.

The balance sheet reports balances of shareholders' equity accounts. In addition, companies also disclose the reasons for *changes* in those accounts. The statement of shareholders' equity serves that purpose. It reports the transactions that cause changes in shareholders' equity account balances.

Illustration

Variety Brands Corporation
Statements of Shareholders' Equity
For the Years Ended Dec. 31, 2003, 2004, 2005 (In millions)

	Common Stock	Additional Paid-in Capital	Retained Earnings	Treasury Stock	Shareholders' Equity
Balance, Jan. 1, 2003	$30	$400	$250	$(180)	$500
Net income	–	–	40	–	40
Cash dividends	–	–	(25)	–	(25)
Common shares sold	5	60	–	–	65
Balance, Dec. 31, 2003	35	460	265	(180)	580
Net income	–	–	50	–	50
Cash dividends	–	–	(35)	–	(35)
Treasury shares	–	–	–	(20)	(20)
Balance, Dec. 31, 2004	35	460	280	(200)	575
Net income	–	–	55	–	55
Cash dividends	–	–	(35)	–	(35)
Balance, Dec. 31, 2005	$35	$460	$300	$(200)	$595

PART B: PAID-IN CAPITAL

Fundamental Share Rights

Common Stock

Ownership rights held by common shareholders usually include:
 a. The right to vote.
 b. The right to share in profits when dividends are declared.
 c. The right to share in the distribution of assets if the company is liquidated.

Preferred Stock

The special rights of preferred shareholders often include one or both of the following:
 a. A preference to a specified amount of dividends so that if the board of directors declares dividends, preferred shareholders receive the designated dividend before any dividends are paid to common shareholders.
 b. A preference (over common shareholders) as to the distribution of assets in the event the corporation is dissolved.

If preferred shares are not cumulative, dividends not declared in any given year need never be paid. If preferred shares are not "participating," shareholders are entitled to no more than the designated dividend preference.

The Concept of Par Value

Assigning a par value to shares has little significance other than historical. Although par value originally indicated the actual value of shares, this is no longer the case. Companies commonly assign shares a nominal par value to dodge elaborate statutory rules pertaining to par value shares. From an accounting perspective, we need to be concerned only that when shares are issued, we record the par amount in common stock, the remainder of the proceeds in additional paid-in capital.

Accounting for the Issuance of Shares

Shares Sold for Cash

When shares are sold for cash, shareholders' investment is allocated between stated capital and additional paid-in capital:

Cash (proceeds from sale)...	xxx	
Common stock (par amount of shares)		xxx
Paid-in capital – excess of par (remainder)..		xxx

Shares Sold on Credit

When shares are sold by share purchase contract, in essence they are sold on credit. Ordinarily the subscriber provides a promissory note. Recording the sale of shares is modified only by including a receivable for the portion of the selling price not yet received.

Cash (proceeds received now)	xxx	
Receivable from share purchase contract (not yet received)........................	xxx	
Common stock (par amount of shares)		xxx
Paid-in capital – excess of par (remainder)...		xxx

Current practice follows an SEC requirement that a receivable from stock sale be reported as a reduction of paid-in capital rather than an asset.

Shares Sold for Noncash Consideration

Occasionally, shares are sold for consideration other than cash, maybe services or a noncash asset. In those instances, the transaction should be recorded at the fair market value of the shares or the noncash consideration, whichever seems more clearly evident. This is consistent with the general rule for accounting for any noncash transaction.

Share Issue Costs

Share issue costs refer to the costs of obtaining the legal, promotional, and accounting services necessary to effect the sale of shares. The costs reduce the net cash proceeds from selling the shares and thus paid-in capital – excess of par, and are not recorded separately.

Reacquired Shares

Companies sometimes reacquire shares previously sold. There is a variety of reasons why, but the most common motivation is to support the market price of the shares. Although, all share repurchases are functionally the same, accounting treatment depends on whether the company states that it is formally retiring the shares or purchasing treasury shares.

Shares Formally Retired

When a corporation retires previously issued shares, those shares assume the same status as authorized but unissued shares – just the same as if they never had been issued. Payments made to retire shares are viewed as a distribution of corporate assets to shareholders. We reduce precisely the same accounts that previously were increased when the shares were sold – namely, common (or preferred) stock and paid-in capital – excess of par.

Illustration

At the time it retired 1 million common shares, General Retailer's balance sheet included the following:

	($ in millions)
Common stock, 100 million shares at $1 par, ...	$ 100
Paid-in capital – excess of par	500

If shares are bought back in 2003 at $4 per share:

Common stock (1 million shares at $1 par)...	1	
Paid-in capital – excess of par (1 million shares at $5 per share)	5	
Paid-in capital – share repurchase (difference)......................................		2
Cash (cost)		4

If another 1 million shares are bought back in 2005 at $9 per share:

Common stock (1 million shares at $1 par)...	1	
Paid-in capital – excess of par (1 million shares at $5 per share)	5	
Paid-in capital – share repurchase (account balance)..................................	2	
Retained earnings (remaining difference)...	1	
Cash (cost)		9

We treat the difference between the cash paid to buy the shares and the amount the shares originally sold for differently depending on whether that difference is positive (credit) or negative (debit):

a. If a *credit* difference is created as in the first entry, we credit paid in capital – share repurchase.

b. If a *debit* difference is created, we debit retained earnings unless a credit balance already exists in paid-in capital – share repurchase, as in the second entry.

Shares Treated as Treasury Stock

The cost of acquiring the shares is "temporarily" debited to the treasury stock account. Recording the effects on specific shareholders' equity accounts is delayed until later when the shares are reissued. In essence, we view the purchase of treasury stock as a *temporary* reduction of shareholders' equity, which is later reversed when the treasury stock is resold.

Illustration

At the time it purchased 1 million common shares, General Retailer's balance sheet included the following:

	($ in millions)
Common stock, 100 million shares at $1 par, ...	$ 100
Paid-in capital – excess of par	500

If shares are bought back in 2003 at $4 per share:		
Treasury stock (cost)	4	
Cash		4
If the shares are later sold at $5 per share:		
Cash (proceeds from sale)..	5	
Treasury stock (previous cost)		4
Paid-in capital – share repurchase (difference)		1
If, instead, the shares are later sold at $3 per share:		
Cash (proceeds from sale)..	3	
Retained earnings (difference)...	1	
Treasury stock (previous cost)		4

At the time the treasury shares are resold, we treat the difference between the cash received and the amount the shares originally cost differently depending on whether that difference is positive (credit) or negative (debit):

a. If a *credit* difference is created as in the first entry, we credit paid-in capital – share repurchase.
b. If a *debit* difference is created as in the second entry, we debit retained earnings unless a credit balance already exists in paid-in capital – share repurchase (not present in this example).

PART C: RETAINED EARNINGS

In general, retained earnings represents a corporation's accumulated, undistributed or reinvested net income (or net loss). Distributions of earned assets are dividends.

Dividends

Most corporate dividends are paid in cash. At the declaration date, retained earnings is reduced and a liability is recorded. Registered owners of shares on the date of record are entitled to receive the dividend.

Illustration

The board of directors of Marlin Properties declared a cash dividend of $.50 per share on its 50 million shares on March 1. The dividend was payable to shareholders of record March 15, to be paid March 30:

		($ in millions)
March 1 – declaration date		
Retained earnings...	25	
Cash dividends payable (50 million shares at $.50/share)		25
March 15 – date of record		
no entry		
March 30 – payment date		
Cash dividends payable	25	
Cash		25

Property Dividends

Occasionally, a noncash asset is distributed. In that case it is referred to as a property dividend. The fair market value of the assets to be distributed is the amount recorded for a property dividend. Before recording the property dividend, the asset may need to be written up or down to fair market value. This would create a gain or loss.

Stock Dividends

In a stock dividend additional shares of stock are distributed to current shareholders. It's important to note that a stock dividend affects neither the assets nor the liabilities of the firm. And, because each shareholder receives the same *percentage* increase in shares, a shareholder's percentage ownership of the firm remains unchanged.

For a "small" stock dividend (less than 25%), the fair value of the additional shares distributed is transferred from retained earnings to paid-in capital.

Retained earnings (market value of new shares)..	xxx	
Common stock (par value of new shares)...		xxx
Paid-in capital – excess of par (remainder)		xxx

Stock Splits

A stock distribution of 25% or higher is a stock split. If referred to as a "stock split effected in the form of a stock dividend," the par value of the additional shares is reclassified within shareholders' equity:

Paid-in capital – excess of par	xxx
Common stock (par value of new shares)..	xxx

If referred to merely as a stock split, no journal entry is recorded.

Decision-Makers' Perspective

The key to a company's long run survival is profitability. The return on shareholders' equity is a summary measure of profitability popular among investors, common shareholders in particular. This ratio is calculated by dividing net income by average shareholders' equity and measures the ability of company management to generate net income from the resources that owners provide.

To supplement the return on shareholders' equity ratio, analysts frequently use the earnings-price ratio to relate earnings to the market value of equity rather than the book value of equity. This ratio is calculated as the earnings per share divided by the market price per share. A popular variation is the inverse – the price-earnings ratio.

The return to shareholders can be significantly affected by decisions that managers make with regard to shareholders' equity transactions. When a corporation buys back shares of its own stock, for instance, the return on shareholders' equity goes up. However, the buy back of shares uses assets, which reduces the resources available to earn net income in the future.

Dividend decisions should be evaluated in light of prevailing circumstances. When cash is available, management must decide whether shareholders are better off receiving cash dividends or having funds reinvested in the firm.

Appendix 19: Quasi-Reorganizations

When a company undergoes financial difficulties, but has favorable future prospects, it may make use of a quasi-reorganization. The firm writes down inflated asset values and eliminates the accumulated deficit (debit balance in retained earnings) following these procedures:

1. Assets and perhaps liabilities are revalued (up or down) to reflect fair market values with corresponding credits or debits to retained earnings. The deficit usually is temporarily increased by this step.

2. Then the debit balance in retained earnings (deficit) is eliminated against additional paid-in capital. If additional paid-in capital is not sufficient to absorb the entire deficit, a reduction in capital stock may be necessary (with an appropriate restating of the par amount per share).

3. For several years, retained earnings is "dated" to indicate the date the deficit was eliminated and when the new accumulation of earnings began.

SELF-STUDY QUESTIONS AND EXERCISES

Concept Review

1. The two primary sources of shareholders' equity are amounts invested by shareholders in the corporation and amounts earned by the corporation on behalf of its shareholders. Invested capital is reported as _____ and earned capital is reported as _____ .

2. The statement of _____ reports the transactions that cause changes in its shareholders' equity account balances.

3. Typical reasons for changes in shareholders' equity are the sale of additional shares of stock, the acquisition of _____, _____, and the declaration of _____.

4. In the eyes of the law, a _____ is a separate legal entity – separate and distinct from its owners.

5. Limited _____ is perhaps the single most important advantage of corporate organization over a proprietorship or a partnership.

6. _____ companies' shares are held by only a few individuals and are not available to the general public.

7. Corporations are formed in accordance with the corporation laws of individual _____.

8. The typical rights of preferred shares usually include a preference to a predesignated amount of _____ and a preference over _____ shareholders in the distribution of assets in the event the corporation is dissolved.

9. If preferred shares are _____ , when the specified dividend is not paid in a given year, the unpaid dividends must be made up in a later dividend year before any dividends are paid on common shares.

10. _____ was defined by early corporation laws as the amount of net assets not available for distribution to shareholders as dividends or otherwise.

11. In a noncash issuance of shares, the measurement objective is that the transaction should be recorded at _____ .

12. _____ costs reduce the net cash proceeds from selling the shares and thus paid-in capital – excess of par.

13. When shares are retired, common (or preferred) stock and _____ are reduced by the same amounts they were increased by when the shares were originally sold.

14. For a stock dividend of less than ___%, the fair market value of the additional shares distributed is transferred from retained earnings to paid-in capital

15. The effect and maybe the motivation for a 2 for 1 stock split is to reduce the per share market price (by half). This will likely increase the stock's _____.

16. If a stock distribution is referred to as a "stock split effected in the form of a stock dividend," and the per share par value of the shares is not changed, a journal entry is recorded that increases the common stock account by the ___ value of the additional shares.

17. When a company decreases, rather than increases, its outstanding shares a _____ stock split occurs.

18. A _____ allows a company to (1) write down inflated asset values and (2) eliminate an accumulated deficit in retained earnings.

Answers:
1. paid-in capital, retained earnings **2.** shareholders' equity **3.** treasury stock, net income, dividends
4. corporation **5.** liability **6.** Privately-held **7.** states **8.** dividends, common
9. cumulative **10.** Par value **11.** fair value **12.** Share issue **13.** paid-in capital – excess of par **14.** 25
15. marketability **16.** par **17.** reverse **18.** quasi reorganization

REVIEW EXERCISES

Exercise 1

Retained earnings is affected by a variety of accounting transactions. For each of the transactions listed below, indicate by letter whether retained earnings is increased **(I)**, decreased **(D)**, or not affected **(N)**. At the time of each transaction, assume the shareholders' equity of the transacting company includes only common stock, paid-in capital – excess of par, and retained earnings.

Transactions

____ 1. Net income for the year
____ 2. A net loss for the year
____ 3. Declaration of a cash dividend
____ 4. Payment of a previously declared cash dividend
____ 5. Declaration of a property dividend
____ 6. Declaration and distribution of a 5% stock dividend
____ 7. A stock split effected in the form of a stock dividend
____ 8. A stock split in which the par value per share is reduced (not effected in the form of a stock dividend)
____ 9. Retirement of common stock at a cost *less* than the original issue price
____ 10. Retirement of common stock at a cost *greater* than the original issue price
____ 11. Purchase of treasury stock at a cost *less* than the original issue price
____ 12. Purchase of treasury stock at a cost *greater* than the original issue price
____ 13. Sale of treasury stock for *more* than cost
____ 14. Sale of treasury stock for *less* than cost
____ 15. Sale of common stock
____ 16. Issuance of convertible bonds for cash

Answers:							
1.	I.	6.	D.	11.	N		
2.	D.	7.	N or D.	12.	N		
3.	D.	8.	N.	13.	N.		
4.	N.	9.	N.	14.	D.		
5.	D.	10.	D.	15.	N	16.	N

Exercise 2

American Mineral Company provides mineral additives to bottled water companies. American's corporate charter authorized the issuance of 24 million, $1 par common shares. During 2003, its first year of operations, American transacted the following:

January 5	Sold 16 million new common shares at $35 per share
April 11	Repurchased 1 million shares at $40 per share
December 2	Sold 1 million shares at $42 per share

Required:
Prepare journal entries to record each of the three transactions under each of two assumptions: (1) American formally retires the shares it buys back and (2) American views share buybacks as treasury shares.

1. Retirement
January 5   ($ in millions)

April 11

December 2

2. Treasury Stock
January 5   ($ in millions)

April 11

December 2

Solution:

1.   Retirement

January 5   ($ in millions)

Cash (16 million x $35)   560
    Common stock (16 million x $1 par)   16
    Paid-in capital – excess of par (16 million x $34)   544

April 11

Common stock (1 million x $1)   1
Paid-in capital – excess of par (1 million x $34)   34
Retained earnings (to balance)   5
    Cash (1 million shares x $40)   40

December 2

Cash (1 million shares x $42)   42
    Common stock (1 million shares x $1)   1
    Paid-in capital – excess of par (remainder)   41

2.   Treasury Stock

January 5   ($ in millions)

Cash (16 million x $35)   560
    Common stock (16 million x $1 par)   16
    Paid-in capital – excess of par (16 million x $34)   544

April 11

Treasury stock (cost)   40
    Cash (1 million shares x $40)   40

December 2

Cash (1 million shares x $42)   42
    Treasury stock (1 million shares x $40)   40
    Paid-in capital – treasury stock (remainder)   2

Shareholders' Equity

Exercise 3

At the beginning of 2003, the shareholders' equity of Couples Home Services consisted of the following:

30 million shares of $1 par common stock	$ 30
5 million shares of $100 par, 8% cumulative, non-participating preferred stock	500
Paid-in capital – excess of par	570
Retained earnings	200

During 2003, Couples earned $240 million. The company declared and paid the contracted amount of preferred dividends plus $2 per share to common shareholders. No dividends had been declared or paid during 2002. On January 8, Couples distributed a 3 for 2 common stock split effected in the form of a stock dividend and reduced paid-in capital – excess of par by the increase in common stock.

Required:
Calculate the balance in retained earnings to be reported on the 2003 balance sheet.

Solution:		
Beginning balance	$200	
Net income	240	
2003 preferred dividends	(40)	5 million shares x $100 par x 8%
2002 preferred dividends	(40)	
2003 common dividends	(90)	[30 x 150%] x $2
Ending balance	$270	

MULTIPLE CHOICE

Enter the letter corresponding to the response that **best** completes each of the following statements or questions.

____ 1. Encore Industries owned investment securities with a carrying amount of $45 million on August 12. At that time, Encore's board of directors declared a property dividend consisting of these securities. The fair value of the securities was as follows:

Declaration – August 12 $58 million
Record date – September 1   62 million
Distribution date – September 20   60 million

What amount of gain should Encore recognize in earnings in connection with this property dividend?

  a. $0
  b. $13 million
  c. $15 million
  d. $17 million

____ 2. What is the effect of the declaration and subsequent issuance of a 5% stock dividend on each of the following?

	Retained earnings	Paid-in capital
a.	no effect	no effect
b.	no effect	increase
c.	increase	decrease
d.	decrease	increase

____ 3. What is the effect of the declaration and subsequent issuance of a stock split (not effected in the form of a stock dividend) on each of the following?

	Retained earnings	Paid-in capital
a.	no effect	no effect
b.	no effect	increase
c.	increase	decrease
d.	decrease	increase

____ 4. What is the effect of the declaration and subsequent issuance of a stock split (effected in the form of a stock dividend) on each of the following?

	Retained earnings	Paid-in capital
a.	no effect	no effect
b.	no effect	increase
c.	increase	decrease
d.	increase	increase

____ 5. Dunavant Service Company views share repurchases as treasury stock. Dunavant purchased shares and then later sold the shares at more than their acquisition price. What is the effect of the sale of the treasury stock on each of the following?

	Paid-in capital	Retained earnings
a.	increase	increase
b.	increase	no effect
c.	no effect	no effect
d.	no effect	increase

____ 6. Motorsports Company retires shares it buys back. In its first share repurchase transaction, Motorsports purchased stock for more than the price at which the stock was originally issued. What is the effect of the purchase of the stock on each of the following?

	Paid-in capital	Retained earnings
a.	decrease	decrease
b.	decrease	no effect
c.	no effect	no effect
d.	no effect	decrease

____ 7. Gabriel Company views share buybacks as treasury stock. In its first treasury stock transaction, Gabriel purchased treasury stock for more than the price at which the stock was originally issued. What is the effect of the purchase of the treasury stock on each of the following?

	Paid-in capital	Retained earnings
a.	decrease	decrease
b.	decrease	no effect
c.	no effect	no effect
d.	no effect	decrease

____ 8. The balance sheet of Epsom Services included the following shareholders' equity section at December 31, 2003:

($ in millions)

Common stock ($1 par value,
  authorized 100 million shares,
  issued and outstanding 90 million shares) $ 90
Paid-in capital – excess of par   540
Retained earnings   280
   Total shareholders' equity $910

On January 5, 2004, Epsom purchased and retired 1 million shares for $9 million. Immediately after retirement of the shares, the balances in the paid-in capital – excess of par and retained earnings accounts are:

	Paid-in capital – excess of par	**Retained earnings**
a.	$540	$280
b.	$540	$272
c.	$534	$278
d.	$532	$280

____ 9. The balance sheet of Holmes Services included the following shareholders' equity section at December 31, 2003:

($ in millions)

Common stock ($1 par value,
  authorized 100 million shares,
  issued and outstanding 90 million shares) $ 90
Paid-in capital – excess of par   540
Retained earnings   280
   Total shareholders' equity $910

On January 5, 2004, Holmes purchased 1 million treasury shares for $9 million. Immediately after the purchase of the shares, the balances in the paid-in capital– excess of par and retained earnings accounts are:

	Paid-in capital – excess of par	**Retained earnings**
a.	$540	$280
b.	$540	$272
c.	$534	$278
d.	$532	$280

____ 10. Sanderson Sofas, a family-owned corporation, issued 6.75% bonds with a face amount of $12 million, together with 2 million shares of its $1 par value common stock, for a combined cash amount of $22 million. The market value of Sanderson's stock cannot be determined. The bonds would have sold for $9 million if issued separately. Sanderson should record for paid-in capital - excess of par on the transaction in the amount of:
   a. $ 8 million
   b. $ 9 million
   c. $11 million
   d. $13 million

____ 11. Westside Shipping issued "preemptive rights" to its existing shareholders without consideration whereby each shareholder is offered the opportunity to buy a percentage of any new shares issued equal to the percentage of shares he/she owns at the time. When Westside issues the rights, which of the following accounts will be increased?

	Common Stock	Additional Paid-in Capital
a.	Yes	Yes
b.	Yes	No
c.	No	No
d.	No	Yes

____ 12. Treasury stock transactions may cause:
   a. An increase in the balance of retained earnings.
   b. A decrease in the balance of retained earnings.
   c. An increase or a decrease in the amount of net income.
   d. An increase or a decrease in the par value per share

____ 13. Chapman Chairs, a family-owned corporation, declared and distributed a property dividend from its overstocked inventory in place of its usual cash dividend. The inventory's carrying value exceeded its fair value. The excess is:
   a. Not reported.
   b. Reported as an ordinary loss.
   c. Reported as an extraordinary loss, net of income taxes.
   d. Reported as a direct reduction of shareholders' equity.

____ 14. The following data were reported in the shareholders' equity section of the Jetson Company's comparative balance sheets for the years ended December 31:

	($ in millions)	
	2003	**2002**
Common stock, $1 par per share	$306	$300
Paid-in capital – excess of par	174	150
Retained earnings	314	300

During 2003, Jetson declared and paid cash dividends of $45 million. The company also declared and issued a stock dividend. No other changes occurred in shares outstanding during 2003. What was Jetson's net income for 2003?
a. $14 million
b. $59 million
c. $65 million
d. $89 million

____ 15. The corporate charter of Pharaoh Tent Co. authorized the issuance of 6 million, $1 par common shares. During 2003, its first year of operations, Pharaoh had the following transactions:

February 4	sold 4 million shares at $15 per share
October 12	retired 1 million shares at $18 per share
December 30	sold the 1 million shares at $20 per share

What amount should Pharaoh report as additional paid-in capital in its December 31, 2003, balance sheet?
a. $37 million
b. $56 million
c. $58 million
d. $61 million

____ 16. The corporate charter of CD, Inc. authorized the issuance of 6 million, $1 par common shares. During 2003, its first year of operations, CD had the following transactions:

February 4	sold 4 million shares at $15 per share
October 12	purchased 1 million treasury shares at $18 per share
December 30	resold the 1 million treasury shares at $20 per share

What amount should CD report as additional paid-in capital in its December 31, 2003, balance sheet?
a. $37 million
b. $56 million
c. $58 million
d. $61 million

____ 17. At the beginning of 2003, Priester Dental Supplies had outstanding 4 million shares of $100 par, 8% cumulative, non-participating preferred stock and 20 million shares of $1 par common stock. During 2003, Priester declared and paid cash dividends of $100 million. No dividends had been declared or paid during 2002. On January 12, Priester issued a 5% common stock dividend when the quoted market price the common stock was $20 per share. What amount of cash did Priester distribute to common shareholders?
   a. $36 million
   b. $56 million
   c. $68 million
   d. $100 million

____ 18. When the 2003 year began, Senatobia Furniture's shareholders' equity included the following:

	($ in millions)
6 million shares of $1 par common stock	$ 6
Paid-in capital – excess of par	114
1 million shares of $100 par, 9% cumulative,	
non-participating preferred stock	100
Retained earnings	140

The company earned $48 million during 2003. At the end of the year, the board of directors declared and paid the contracted amount of preferred dividends as well as $3 per share to common shareholders. No dividends had been declared or paid during 2002. On January 5, the company distributed a 3 for 2 common stock split effected in the form of a stock dividend. What is the balance in retained earnings to be reported on the 2003 balance sheet?
   a. $143 million
   b. $152 million
   c. $160 million
   d. $188 million

Answers:

1.	b.	6.	a.	11.	c.	16.	c
2.	d.	7.	c.	12.	b.	17.	a
3.	a.	8.	c.	13.	b.	18.	a
4.	a.	9.	a.	14.	d.		
5.	b.	10.	c.	15.	d.		

Earnings per Share

LEARNING OBJECTIVES

After studying this chapter, you should be able to:

1. Distinguish between a simple and a complex capital structure.
2. Describe what is meant by the weighted average number of common shares.
3. Differentiate the effect on EPS of the sale of new shares, a stock dividend or stock split, and the reacquisition of shares.
4. Describe how preferred dividends affect the determination of EPS.
5. Describe how options, rights, and warrants are incorporated in the calculation of EPS.
6. Describe how convertible securities are incorporated in the calculation of EPS.
7. Explain the way contingently issuable shares are incorporated in the calculation of EPS.
8. Describe the financial statement presentation of EPS.

CHAPTER HIGHLIGHTS

A Popular Accounting Number

Earnings per share is the most often cited and most frequently reported measure of a company's performance. EPS is reported on the income statement of all publicly traded firms.

Basic Earnings per Share

In general, EPS is simply earnings available to common shareholders divided by the weighted average number of common shares outstanding.

When "potential common shares" are outstanding, the company is said to have a **complex capital structure**. In that case, two EPS calculations are reported:

➡ Basic EPS assumes no dilution.
➡ Diluted EPS assumes maximum potential dilution.

When a firm has no "potential common shares" it has a **simple capital structure**. In that case, a single presentation of basic EPS is sufficient.

Earnings per Share

Weighted Average Number of Shares

EPS calculations are based on the weighted average number of common shares outstanding during the period. Accordingly, any new shares that are issued during the period are time-weighted by the fraction of the period they were outstanding and then added to the number of shares outstanding for the period.

Illustration

Boston House, a calendar-year firm with 600,000 shares common outstanding sells 60,000 new shares on September 1.

The denominator of the EPS fraction is increased by: $60,000 \times {}^4/_{12}$, or 20,000 shares. The weighted average number of shares outstanding would be 620,000.

Stock Dividend or Stock Split

An increase in shares due to a stock dividend or stock split is handled quite differently as compared to a sale of shares. For a stock dividend or stock split, shares outstanding prior to the stock distribution are retroactively restated to reflect the increase in shares. That is, we simply increase the outstanding shares by the number of new shares. The company is represented by a larger number of less valuable shares. Stated differently, the same pie is cut into more slices. Other things being equal, EPS after a 2 for 1 stock split would be half what EPS was before. In fact, when reported again in the comparative financial statements last year's EPS (and any other years' reported) would be restated for comparability.

Illustration

Boston House, a calendar-year firm with 600,000 common shares outstanding distributes a 10% stock dividend (60,000 shares) on September 1.

The denominator of the EPS fraction is simply increased to 600,000 (1.10), or 660,000 shares. This is the weighted average number of shares outstanding.

Treasury Stock or Retired Shares

When shares are reacquired, as treasury stock or to be retired, they are time-weighted for the fraction of the period they were *not* outstanding, prior to being *subtracted* from the number of shares outstanding during the reporting period.

Illustration

Boston House, a calendar-year firm with 600,000 shares common outstanding retires 60,000 shares on September 1.

The denominator of the EPS fraction is decreased by: $60,000 \times {}^4/_{12}$, or 20,000 shares. The weighted average number of shares common outstanding would be 580,000.

Preferred Dividends

Because the denominator in the EPS calculation is the weighted average number of *common* shares, the numerator should reflect earnings available to *common* shareholders. As a result, any dividends on preferred stock outstanding are subtracted from reported net income. We make this adjustment for *cumulative* preferred stock whether or not dividends are declared that period.

Illustration

Boston House, a calendar-year firm with 600,000 common shares outstanding also has 10,000 shares of 9%, cumulative $100 par preferred stock. Net income was $700,000.

The numerator of the EPS fraction is decreased by: $10,000 \times \$100 \times 9\%$, or $90,000. The numerator, earnings available to common shareholders, would be $610,000 ($700,000 - 90,000).

Diluted Earnings per Share

If a firm's capital structure includes securities that could potentially dilute (reduce) earnings per share (such as convertible securities or stock options), it is classified as a complex capital structure and the company reports both **basic** and **diluted** earnings per share. The impact of each "potential common share" is reflected by calculating earnings per share as if the security already had been exercised or converted into additional common shares.

Stock Options (or Rights or Warrants)

Stock options, as well as stock rights and stock warrants, give their holders the right to exercise their option to purchase common stock, usually at a specified *exercise price*. The resulting increase in shares would reduce EPS. For diluted EPS, we pretend that stock options, rights, and warrants were exercised at the beginning of the period (or at the time the options are issued, if later). We also assume the cash proceeds received are used to buy back (as treasury stock) as many of those shares as could be acquired at the average market price during the period.

Illustration

Boston House, a calendar-year firm with 600,000 common shares outstanding also has at year-end executive stock options outstanding permitting executives to buy 60,000 shares of stock for $25. The average price of the shares during the year was $30.

We pretend 60,000 shares were sold for $25 per share at the beginning of the year and the cash proceeds were used to buy back as many of those shares as could be bought for $30. The 50,000 shares assumed reacquired are calculated as:

	60,000	option shares
x	$25	(exercise price)
	$1,500,000	cash proceeds
÷	$30	(average market price)
	50,000	shares assumed reacquired

The denominator of the diluted EPS fraction is increased by: 60,000 minus 50,000, or 10,000 shares. The denominator would be 610,000. Basic EPS is unaffected.

Note: If the stock options had been granted on July first of the year just ended, the options would be assumed exercised on July 1 and the additional shares would be time-weighted as follows: $10,000 \times {}^{6}/_{12}$, 5,000.

Convertible Bonds

To represent convertible bonds in the calculation of diluted EPS, we pretend the conversion occurred at the beginning of the period (or at the time the convertible security is issued, if later). The denominator of the EPS fraction is adjusted for the additional common shares assumed and the numerator is increased by the interest (after-tax) that would have been avoided in the event of conversion.

Illustration

Boston House, a calendar-year firm with 600,000 common shares outstanding also has at year-end $1,000,000 of 9% convertible bonds sold at face value three years ago, permitting investors to exchange their bonds for 60,000 shares of stock.

We pretend the bonds were converted and 60,000 shares were issued at the beginning of the year. We would simply add the 60,000 shares to the denominator. The numerator would be increased by the after-tax interest that was paid to bondholders but would not have been paid if the bonds had been converted. The increase, assuming a 40% tax rate would be $54,000:

$1,000,000	face amount of bonds
x ____9%	interest rate
$90,000	reduction in interest expense and increase in pretax income
(36,000)	$90,000 x 40%
$54,000	after-tax interest savings

If net income had been $700,000, EPS would have been:

$$\text{Basic:} \quad \frac{\$700,000}{600,000} = {} = \$1.17$$

$$\text{Diluted:} \quad \frac{\$700,000 + \$90,000 - (\$90,000 \times 40\%)}{600,000 + 60,000} = \frac{\$754,000}{660,000} = \$1.14$$

Convertible Preferred Shares

To represent convertible preferred stock in the calculation of diluted EPS, we pretend the conversion occurred at the beginning of the period (or at the time the convertible preferred stock was issued, if later). The denominator of the EPS fraction is adjusted for the additional common shares assumed and the numerator is increased by the preferred dividends that would have been avoided in the event of conversion.

Illustration

Boston House, a calendar-year firm with 600,000 common shares outstanding also has at year-end $500,000 of 8% convertible, cumulative preferred stock sold at face value three years ago, permitting investors to exchange their preferred shares for 60,000 shares of common stock.

We pretend the preferred shares were converted and 60,000 common shares were issued at the beginning of the year. We would simply add the 60,000 shares to the denominator. The numerator would be increased by the preferred dividends that would not have been paid if the preferred shares had been converted. If net income had been $700,000, EPS would have been:

$$\textbf{Basic:} \quad \frac{\$700{,}000 - \$40{,}000^{*}}{600{,}000} = \frac{\$660{,}000}{600{,}000} = \$1.10$$

$$\textbf{Diluted:} \quad \frac{\$700{,}000 - \$40{,}000^{*} + \$40{,}000^{*}}{600{,}000 + 60{,}000} = \frac{\$700{,}000}{660{,}000} = \$1.06$$

* $500,000 x 8%

Contingently Issuable Shares

Contingently issuable shares are considered outstanding in the computation of *diluted* EPS when the conditions for their issuance are currently met. For instance, if 60,000 shares will be issued next year if net income next year is at least $600,000 and this year's net income is $700,000, the presumption is that next year's net income will be at least as high and the 60,000 additional shares would be simply added to the denominator.

Antidilutive Securities

When the effect of the assumed conversion or exercise of potential common shares would be to increase, rather than decrease, EPS, we deem them "antidilutive securities." Antidilutive securities are ignored when calculating both basic and diluted EPS.

EPS Disclosures

EPS, both basic and diluted, are reported separately for income from continuing operations and net income. Per share amounts for discontinued operations, extraordinary items, and an accounting change also are reported. Disclosures should include a reconciliation of the numerator and denominator used in the computations.

Decision-Makers' Perspective

A common way decision makers use EPS data is in connection with the price-earnings ratio. This is the market price per share divided by the earning per share. The P/E ratio measures the decision makers' perception of the "quality" of a company's earnings. It indicates the price multiple the market is willing to pay for the firm's earnings. Accordingly, it represents the market's expectation of *future* earnings as indicated by current earnings. In a real sense, this ratio reflects the information provided by all available information because the market price reflects analysts' perceptions of a business's growth potential, stability, and relative risk.

Another measure, the dividend payout ratio denotes the percentage of earnings that is distributed to shareholders as dividends.

Earnings per Share

SELF-STUDY QUESTIONS AND EXERCISES

Concept Review

1. When the capital structure includes securities other than common stock the firm is said to have a _____ capital structure.
2. Willingham Company began the 2003 calendar year with 10 million common shares outstanding, but on September 30 sold one million additional shares. Willingham's weighted average number of shares outstanding would be _____ shares.
3. If a business has potential common shares outstanding, two EPS calculations are reported. _____ EPS assumes no dilution. _____ EPS assumes maximum potential dilution.
4. EPS calculations are based on the weighted average number of shares outstanding during the period. Any new shares issued during the period are time-weighted by the _____ of the period they were outstanding and then added to the number of shares outstanding for the period.
5. When calculating the weighted average number of shares outstanding, common shares issued in a stock _____ or stock _____ are not weighted by the fraction of the period they are outstanding.
6. If shares are reacquired, either as treasury stock or to be retired, they are time-weighted for the fraction of the period they were not outstanding, prior to being _____ the number of shares outstanding during the period.
7. Dividends on _____ outstanding should be subtracted from reported net income.
8. For diluted EPS, we assume stock options were exercised at the beginning of the period and that the cash proceeds received were used to buy back as many of those shares as can be acquired at the _____ price during the period.
9. To include convertible bonds in the calculation of diluted EPS, the denominator of the EPS fraction is adjusted for the _____ and the numerator is increased by the _____ that would have been avoided in the event of conversion.
10. _____ shares are considered outstanding in the computation of *diluted* EPS when they will later be issued because of conditions for issuance currently are met.
11. EPS data (both basic and diluted) must be reported separately for income from _____ and _____ .
12. If a firm does not declare dividends on preferred stock, an adjustment of the numerator is required in earnings per share calculations if the preferred stock is _____ .

Answers:
1. complex **2.** 10,250,000 **3.** Basic, Diluted **4.** fraction **5.** dividend, split **6.** subtracted from **7.** preferred stock **8.** average market **9.** additional common shares, after-tax interest **10.** Contingently issuable **11.** continuing operations , net income **12.** cumulative

REVIEW EXERCISES

Exercise 1

On January 1, 2003, Landover Bicycle Company had outstanding 200 million shares of common stock and 20 million shares of 7.5% cumulative preferred stock (par $10).

On March 1, 2003, Landover sold and issued an additional 24 million shares of common stock. The company distributed a 10% common stock dividend on May 5. On November 1, six million shares were retired in keeping with the company's long-term share repurchase plan.

Net income was $465 million. The tax rate for the year was 40%.

Required: Compute EPS for the year ended December 31, 2003.

Solution:

($ in millions, except per share amounts)

Basic EPS

$$\frac{\overset{\substack{\text{net}\\\text{income}}}{\$465} \overset{\substack{\text{preferred}\\\text{dividends}}}{-\ \$15*}}{\underset{\substack{\text{shares}\\\text{at Jan. 1}}}{200\ (1.10)} + \underset{\substack{\text{new}\\\text{shares}}}{24\ (^{10}/_{12})\ (1.10)} - \underset{\substack{\text{retired}\\\text{shares}}}{6\ (^{2}/_{12})}} = \frac{\$450}{241} = \$1.87$$

↑__stock dividend __↑
adjustment

*$10 x 20 million shares x 7.5%

Earnings per Share

Exercise 2

In addition to the information provided in Exercise 1, assume the following additional items for Landover:

- At year-end, there were executive stock options outstanding for 12 million shares of common stock (adjusted for the stock dividend). The exercise price was $25. The market price of the common stock during the year had averaged $30.

- Also outstanding were $600 million face amount of 10% convertible bonds issued in 2001 and convertible into 24 million common shares (adjusted for the stock dividend).

Required: Compute basic and diluted EPS for the year ended December 31, 2003.

Solution:

($ in millions, except per share amounts)

Basic EPS

net income	preferred dividends	
$465	− $15	

$$\frac{\$465 \quad -\$15}{200 \,(1.10) \;+\; 24 \,(^{10}/_{12})(1.10) \;-\; 6\,(^{2}/_{12})} = \frac{\$450}{241} = \$1.87$$

200 (1.10) — shares at Jan. 1
+ 24 ($^{10}/_{12}$)(1.10) — new shares
− 6 ($^{2}/_{12}$) — retired shares
↑__stock dividend __↑ adjustment

$450

241

Diluted EPS

net income	preferred dividends	after-tax Interest savings
$465	− $15	+ $60 - (40% x $60)

$$\frac{\$465 \quad -\$15 \quad +\$60-(40\% \times \$60)}{200\,(1.10)\;+\;24\,(^{10}/_{12})(1.10)\;-\;6\,(^{2}/_{12})\;+\;(12-10^{*})\;+\;24} = \frac{\$486}{267} = \$1.82$$

200 (1.10) — shares at Jan. 1
+ 24 ($^{10}/_{12}$)(1.10) — new shares
− 6 ($^{2}/_{12}$) — retired shares
+ (12 − 10*) — exercise of options
+ 24 — conversion of bonds
↑__stock dividend __↑ adjustment

$486

267

*Shares Reacquired for Basic EPS

	12	million shares
x	$25	(exercise price)
	$300	million
÷	$30	(average market price)
	10	million shares reacquired

Exercise 3

Assume the convertible bonds in Exercise 2 were convertible into 10 million common shares rather than 24 million shares.

Required: Compute diluted EPS for the year ended December 31, 2003.

Solution:

When the effect of the assumed conversion would be to increase, rather than decrease, EPS, they are considered "antidilutive securities." Antidilutive securities are ignored when calculating both basic and diluted EPS. This is the case with the convertible bonds. Including the conversion would cause EPS to **increase** to $1.92:

($ in millions, except per share amount)

Diluted EPS

$$\frac{\underset{\substack{\text{net} \\ \text{income}}}{\$465} \quad \underset{\substack{\text{preferred} \\ \text{dividends}}}{-\ \$15} \quad \underset{\substack{\text{after-tax} \\ \text{Interest savings}}}{+\ \$60 - 40\%\ (\$60)}}{\underset{\substack{\text{shares} \\ \text{at Jan. 1}}}{200\ (1.10)} \ + \underset{\substack{\text{new} \\ \text{shares}}}{24\ (^{10}/_{12})\ (1.10)} \ - \underset{\substack{\text{retired} \\ \text{shares}}}{6\ (^{2}/_{12})} \ + \underset{\substack{\text{exercise} \\ \text{of options}}}{(12 - 10)} \ + \underset{\substack{\text{conversion} \\ \text{of bonds}}}{10}} = \frac{\$486}{253} = \$1.92$$

↑___stock dividend ___↑
adjustment

As a result, we ignore the conversion when calculating EPS:

Diluted EPS

$$\frac{\underset{\substack{\text{net} \\ \text{income}}}{\$465} \quad \underset{\substack{\text{preferred} \\ \text{dividends}}}{-\ \$15}}{\underset{\substack{\text{shares} \\ \text{at Jan. 1}}}{200\ (1.10)} \ + \underset{\substack{\text{new} \\ \text{shares}}}{24\ (^{10}/_{12})\ (1.10)} \ - \underset{\substack{\text{retired} \\ \text{shares}}}{6\ (^{2}/_{12})} \ + \underset{\substack{\text{exercise} \\ \text{of options}}}{(12 - 10)}} = \frac{\$450}{243} = \$1.85$$

↑___stock dividend ___↑
adjustment

Earnings per Share

MULTIPLE CHOICE

Enter the letter corresponding to the response that **best** completes each of the following statements or questions.

___ 1. Which of the following statements is **untrue** regarding earnings per share?
   a. A company has a simple capital structure if it has no outstanding securities that could potentially dilute earnings per share.
   b. When shares are retired, they are time-weighted for the fraction of the period they were not outstanding, prior to being subtracted from the number of shares outstanding during the reporting period.
   c. Dividends paid on nonconvertible preferred stock outstanding should be subtracted from reported net income.
   d. Any new shares issued during the period in a stock dividend or stock split are time-weighted by the fraction of the period they were outstanding and then added to the number of shares outstanding for the period.

___ 2. At December 31, 2003 and 2004, Frist Company had outstanding 50 million common shares and 4 million shares of 10%, $10 par cumulative preferred stock. Net income for 2004 was $20 million. No dividends were declared in 2003 or 2004. EPS for 2004 was:
   a. $.32.
   b. $.37.
   c. $.40.
   d. $.48.

___ 3. At December 31, 2003, the balance sheet of Goode Corporation included 80 million common shares. On October 1, 2004, Goode retired 4 million shares as part of a share repurchase program. Net income for the year ended December 31, 2004, was $400 million. Goode's 2004 EPS should be:
   a. $4.94.
   b. $5.00.
   c. $5.06.
   d. $5.26.

___ 4. At December 31, 2003, the balance sheet of Darwin Corporation included 8 million common shares and 4 million nonconvertible preferred shares. On July 1, 2004, Darwin issued a 5 for 4 stock split on its common shares and paid $10 million cash dividends on the preferred stock. Net income for the year ended December 31, 2004, was $40 million. Darwin's 2004 EPS should be:
   a. $3.00.
   b. $4.00.
   c. $5.00.
   d. $5.55.

_____ 5. When calculating basic earnings per share, net income is reduced by dividends on nonconvertible cumulative preferred stock:
   a. Whether declared or not.
   b. Only if declared.
   c. Whether dilutive or not.
   d. Under no circumstances.

_____ 6. When calculating the weighted average number of shares outstanding, the number of shares are **not** time-weighted by the fraction of the reporting period they are (are not) outstanding for:
   a. Common shares retired.
   b. Common shares issued during the period as a stock dividend.
   c. Shares obtainable in executive stock options granted in mid-year.
   d. New common shares sold during the period.

_____ 7. A business is deemed to have a complex capital structure when it has outstanding:
   a. Three types of securities or more besides common stock.
   b. Executive stock options.
   c. Bonds payable.
   d. Cumulative preferred stock.

_____ 8. To incorporate the effect of outstanding stock options in the calculation of diluted EPS:
   a. Would be inappropriate because options are considered only when calculating basic EPS.
   b. We would never increase or decrease the numerator of the EPS fraction.
   c. We assume common shares are issued at the average market price and repurchased at the exercise price.
   d. We assume the options were exercised at mid-year.

_____ 9. When calculating diluted EPS, which of the following, if dilutive, would cause the weighted average number of shares to increase?

	Dividends on preferred stock	**Stock options**
a.	Yes	No
b.	Yes	Yes
c.	No	Yes
d.	No	No

___ 10. When calculating earnings per share, the effect of after-tax interest expense paid on convertible bonds that are dilutive is to:
   a. Increase net income for diluted earnings per share and not for basic earnings per share.
   b. Decrease net income for basic earnings per share and not for diluted earnings per share.
   c. Increase net income for both basic earnings per share and diluted earnings per share.
   d. Decrease net income for both basic earnings per share and diluted earnings per share.

___ 11. Common stock options that are antidilutive generally affect the calculation of:

	Basic EPS	Diluted EPS
a.	Yes	Yes
b.	Yes	No
c.	No	No
d.	No	Yes

___ 12. Convertible bonds that are dilutive generally affect the calculation of:

	Basic EPS	Diluted EPS
a.	Yes	Yes
b.	Yes	No
c.	No	No
d.	No	Yes

___ 13. Executive stock options are outstanding all year that permit executives to buy 12 million common shares at $50. The average market price of the common stock was $60. When calculating diluted earnings per share, the assumed exercise of these options will increase the weighted average number of shares outstanding by:
   a.   zero shares.
   b.   2 million shares.
   c.   8 million shares.
   d.   10 million shares.

___ 14. Executive stock options are outstanding all year that permit executives to buy 12 million common shares at $60. The average market price of the common stock was $50. When calculating diluted earnings per share, the assumed exercise of these options will increase the weighted average number of shares outstanding by:
   a.   zero shares.
   b.   2 million shares.
   c.   8 million shares.
   d.   10 million shares.

___ 15. Which of the following statements is **true** regarding diluted earnings per share?
   a. It is assumed that stock options are exercised at the beginning of the period (or at the time the options are issued, if later) and the cash proceeds received are used to buy back (as treasury stock) as many of those shares as can be acquired at the closing market price for the period.
   b. To incorporate convertible bonds into the calculation, the denominator of the EPS fraction is decreased by the additional common shares assumed.
   c. To incorporate convertible securities into the calculation, the numerator is decreased by the interest (after-tax) that would have been avoided in the event of conversion.
   d. Contingently issuable shares are considered outstanding in the computation of *diluted* EPS when any conditions for issuance are currently being met.

___ 16. Which of the following is **not** disclosed regarding earnings per share?
   a. Basic EPS for income from continuing operations.
   b. Diluted EPS for net income.
   c. Cash paid per share.
   d. Reconciliation of the numerator and denominator used in the computations.

Answers:

1.	d	6.	b	11.	c	16.	c
2.	a	7.	b	12.	d		
3.	c	8.	b	13.	b		
4.	a	9.	c	14.	a		
5.	a	10.	a	15.	d		

Accounting Changes and Error Corrections

LEARNING OBJECTIVES

After studying this chapter, you should be able to:

1. Differentiate among the three types of accounting changes and distinguish among the retroactive, current, and prospective approaches to accounting for and reporting accounting changes.
2. Determine the cumulative effect of an accounting change and describe how changes in accounting principle typically are reported.
3. Explain how and why some changes in accounting principle are reported retroactively or prospectively.
4. Explain how and why changes in estimates are reported prospectively
5. Describe the situations that constitute a change in reporting entity.
6. Understand and apply the four-step process of correcting and reporting errors, regardless of the type of error or the timing of its discovery.

CHAPTER HIGHLIGHTS

PART A: ACCOUNTING CHANGES

Types of Accounting Changes

For accounting purposes, we identify three types of accounting changes:

❖ Changes in *principle*.
❖ Changes in *estimates*.
❖ Changes in *reporting entity*.

Accounting changes can be accounted for:

❖ *Retroactively* (prior years restated)
❖ *Currently* (cumulative effect reported currently)
❖ *Prospectively* (only current and future years affected)

The choice depends on the type of change.

Changes in Accounting Principle

Although consistency and comparability are desirable, changing from one accounting method to another method sometimes is appropriate. This is called a change in accounting principle.

GENERAL APPROACH

Most changes in accounting principle are recorded and reported by the *current approach*. By this approach, the *cumulative income effect* (net of the tax impact) is reported as a separate item of income between extraordinary items and net income.

Illustration

In 2004, the Arizona Company changed its method of valuing inventory from the average cost method to the FIFO method. At December 31, 2003, Arizona's inventories were $35 million (average cost). Arizona's accounting records indicated that the inventories would have totaled $45 million on that date if determined on a FIFO basis. Arizona's tax rate is 40%.

	($ in millions)
The journal entry to record the adjustment:	
Inventory ($45 million – $35 million) 10	
Deferred tax liability ($10 x 40%)	4
Cumulative effect of accounting change (difference)	6

In prior years, inventory would have been $10 million higher by FIFO, and cost of goods sold would have been $10 million lower. Thus, pretax income would have been $10 million higher. However, with a 40% tax rate, net income would have been higher by only $6 million. This is the cumulative effect of the accounting change.

The reason for the credit to deferred tax liability requires you to reflect back on what you learned about accounting for income taxes. Also remember that changing inventory methods for financial reporting requires the same change for tax purposes. The Internal Revenue Code requires that taxes saved previously from having used another inventory method ($4 million in this case) must now be repaid (over no longer than 6 years). In the meantime, there is temporary book-tax difference for the inventory account, reflected in the deferred tax liability.

The cumulative income effect is reported as a separate item of income between extraordinary items and net income.

Reported as a separate component of income:

	2004	2003
	($ in millions)	
Income before extraordinary items and accounting change	$xxx	$xxx
Extraordinary gain (loss), net of tax	xx	xx
Cumulative effect of accounting change (net of $4 tax)	**6**	
Net income	$xxx	$xxx

→ The effect of the change on certain key income numbers should be disclosed for the current period as well as on a "pro forma" basis for all prior periods that are included for comparison with the current financial statements.

→ The nature of and justification for the change, as well as the effect on current earnings, should be described in a disclosure note as well.

EXCEPTIONS – RETROACTIVE APPROACH

Because of their unique nature, prior years' financial statements are *restated* to reflect some changes in accounting principle. These exceptions to the general approach are:

1. Those required by a specific accounting standard.
   a. Some FASB Statements require retroactive application for the initial transition to the new standards.
   b. Some FASB Statements and other authoritative pronouncements require retroactive application for specific changes in accounting methods. (i.e. change from the cost method to the equity method of accounting for long-term investments)
2. A change from the LIFO method to another inventory valuation method.
3. A change from the percentage of completion to the completed contract method (or vice versa) in accounting for long-term construction contracts.
4. A change to or from the "full cost" method in the oil and gas and other extractive industries.
5. Changes made when a closely-held corporation first issues financial statements to obtain equity financing, for registering securities, or for effecting a business combination.

These five exceptions receive special accounting treatment. Financial statements of prior years are restated for the effect of the change, rather than reporting that effect as part of income in the year the change occurs. The main reason is that the effect of these changes usually is quite large.

EXCEPTIONS – PROSPECTIVE APPROACH

Also, a change to LIFO and a few changes mandated by new accounting standards are accounted for *prospectively*. For example, when a company changes to the LIFO method, accounting records of prior years usually are inadequate to determine what the LIFO layers would have been or the cumulative income effect of the change. So, we simply begin using LIFO from that point on. The base year inventory for all future LIFO calculations is the beginning inventory in the year the LIFO method is adopted. Also, a disclosure note should explain the change and how it is handled.

Changes in Estimate

Estimates are commonplace in accounting. Depreciation, for example, involves estimating, not only of the useful lives of depreciable assets, but also their anticipated salvage values. Inevitably, though, many estimates turn out to be incorrect, forcing the revision of estimates. This is called a change in estimate.

Because revisions are viewed as a natural consequence of making estimates, when a company revises a previous estimate, prior financial statements are *not* restated. Furthermore, the cumulative effect of the change is not included in current income. Instead, the company simply incorporates the new estimate in any related accounting determinations from that point on.

Illustration

The Wireless Company has a patent on a wireless internet connection process. Wireless has amortized the patent on a straight-line basis since 2001, when it was acquired at a cost of $16 million at the beginning of that year. Recent technological advances in the industry caused management to decide that the patent would benefit the company over a total of five years rather than the 8-year life being used to amortize its cost. The decision was made at the end of 2003 (before adjusting and closing entries).

The journal entry to record the adjustment:	($ in millions)	
Patent amortization expense (determined below)	4	
Patent		4

Calculation of annual amortization after the estimate change:

	($ in millions)	
	$16	Cost
$2		Old annual amortization ($16 ÷ 8 years)
x 2 years	(4)	Amortization to date (2001-2002)
	$12	Unamortized cost (balance in the patent account)
	÷ 3	Estimated remaining life (5 years – 2 years)
	$ 4	New annual amortization

Changes in Reporting Entity

A reporting entity can be a single company. Also a group of companies that reports a single set of financial statements can be a reporting entity. Occasionally, changes occur that cause the financial statements to be those of a different reporting entity. This occurs as a result of:

❖ Presenting consolidated financial statements in place of statements of individual companies,

❖ Changing specific companies that comprise the group for which consolidated or combined statements are prepared, or

❖ A business combination accounted for as a pooling of interests.

A change in reporting entity is accounted for retroactively. That is, financial statements of prior periods are restated to report the financial information for the new reporting entity in all periods.

PART B: CORRECTION OF ERRORS

Mistakes happen. When errors are discovered, they should be corrected and accounted for retroactively. Previous years' financial statements that were incorrect as a result of an error are retroactively restated, and any account balances that are incorrect are corrected by a journal entry. If retained earnings is one of the accounts incorrect, the correction is reported as a "prior period adjustment" to the beginning balance in a statement of shareholders' equity. And, a disclosure note should describe the nature of the error and the impact of its correction on operations.

❖ A journal entry is recorded to correct any account balances that are incorrect as a result of the error.

❖ If the error created an incorrect balance in retained earnings, the correction is reported as an adjustment to the beginning balance in a statement of retained earnings, or statement of shareholders' equity.

❖ Prior years' financial statements are restated to eliminate the error (if the error affected those statements).

❖ A disclosure note should report the nature of the error and the impact of its correction on net income, income before extraordinary items, and earnings per share.

To determine which balances are in need of correction, it's helpful to write down the entry(s) made and those that should have been made. Comparing the correct and incorrect entries can simplify the analysis.

Illustration

The Diversified Company purchased a five-year casualty insurance policy at the beginning of 2004 for $450,000. The full amount was debited to insurance expense at the time. Th error was discovered in January of 2006.

Analysis:

	Correct (Should Have Been Recorded)		Incorrect (As Recorded)	
2004 Prepaid insurance	450,000		Insurance expense	450,000
Cash		450,000	Cash		450,000
2004 Insurance expense	90,000		Adjusting entry omitted	
Prepaid insurance		90,000		
2005 Insurance expense	90,000		Adjusting entry omitted	
Prepaid insurance		90,000		

If recorded correctly, during the two year period insurance expense would have been $180,000. Instead, it was $450,000. Expenses, therefore, were *overstated* by $270,000, so net income during the period was *understated* by $270,000. Ignoring taxes, this means retained earnings is currently *understated* by that amount.

Also, prepaid insurance should have a balance of $270,000 ($450,000 - 90,000 - 90,000).

The journal entry to correct the error:

Prepaid insurance	270,000	
Retained earnings		270,000

❖ The financial statements the last two years that were incorrect as a result of the error would be retroactively restated to report the prepaid insurance acquired and reflect the correct amount of insurance expense when those statements are reported again for comparative purposes in the current annual report.

❖ A "prior period adjustment" to retained earnings would be reported

❖ A disclosure note should describe the nature of the error and the impact of its correction on each year's net income, income before extraordinary items, and earnings per share.

SELF-STUDY QUESTIONS AND EXERCISES

Concept Review

1. Accounting changes are categorized as changes in _____, or _____, or _____.

2. Changes in _____ occur when companies switch from one acceptable accounting method to another.

3. Changes in _____ occur when new information causes companies to revise estimates made previously.

4. Changes in _____ occur when the group of companies comprising the reporting entity changes.

5. Accounting changes can be accounted for _____ (prior years restated), _____ (cumulative effect reported currently), or _____ (only current and future years affected).

6. Most changes in accounting principles are recorded and reported by the "current approach." The cumulative income effect, net of _____ is reported as a separate item of income.

7. The cumulative income effect is reported on the income statement between _____ and net income.

8. The effect of a change in accounting principle on certain key income numbers should be reported for the _____ and on a "pro forma" ("as if") basis for the financial statements of _____.

9. The nature of and justification for a change in accounting principle, as well as the effect on current earnings, should be described in _____.

10. When a cumulative effect type change in accounting principle is made during the year, the cumulative effect on retained earnings is determined as of _____.

11. A few changes in accounting principles are recorded and reported retroactively. A retroactive change involving a change in inventory method is a change from the _____ method to another inventory valuation method.

12. When it's not possible to distinguish between a change in principle and a change in estimate, the change should be treated as a change in _____.

13. When an error is discovered, previous years' financial statements that were incorrect as a result of the error are _____ to reflect the correction.

14. When an error is discovered, any account balances that currently are incorrect as a result of the error should be corrected by a journal entry. If retained earnings is one of the accounts whose balance is incorrect, the correction is reported as a _____ to the beginning balance in a statement of shareholders' equity (or statement of retained earnings if that's presented instead).

15. If merchandise inventory is understated at the end of 2003, 2003's cost of goods sold would be ___, causing 2003 net income to be _____.

Accounting Changes and Error Correction

Answers:
1. principle, estimate, reporting entity **2.** principle **3.** estimate **4.** reporting entity
5. retroactively, currently, prospectively **6.** the tax effect **7.** extraordinary items **8.** current period, all prior periods included in the report **9.** a disclosure note **10.** the beginning of the year in which the change is made **11.** LIFO **12.** estimate **13.** retroactively restated **14.** prior period adjustment **15.** overstated, understated

REVIEW EXERCISES

Exercise 1
At the beginning of 2002, Risk Management Corporation purchased copy equipment for $900,000. The equipment's useful life was estimated to be 10 years with no salvage value and has been depreciated by the double-declining balance method. On January 1, 2004, management changed retroactively to the straight-line method. The effective income tax rate is 40%.

Required:
1. Determine the cumulative effect of the change in depreciation method.

2. Prepare the journal entry to record the cumulative effect of the change in depreciation method.

3. Prepare the adjusting entry to record depreciation for 2004.

Solution:

1. Cumulative effect of the change ($ in 000s):

	DDB	**Straight-line**
2002 depreciation	$180 ($900 x 20%)	$ 90 ($900 ÷ 10)
2003 depreciation	144 ($720 x 20%)	90 ($900 ÷ 10)
Accumulated depreciation and		
2002-2003 reduction in pretax income	$324	$180

$$\searrow \quad \text{difference} \quad \swarrow$$
$$\$144.0$$

Tax (40% x $144)   (57.6)

$ 86.4

2. To record the change:

Accumulated depreciation	144,000	
Deferred tax liability ($144,000 x 40%)		57,600
Cumulative effect of accounting change		86,400

3. 2004 adjusting entry:

Depreciation expense ($900,000 ÷ 10 years)	90,000	
Accumulated depreciation		90,000

Exercise 2

Ballpark Awnings estimates bad debt expense as 3% of credit sales. After a review during 2003, Ballpark decided that 2% of credit sales is a more realistic estimate of its collection practices. Ballpark's credit sales in 2003 were $25 million. The effective income tax rate is 40%.

Required:

1. By what amounts are bad debt expense and the allowance for uncollectible accounts reported last year restated?

2. What is the cumulative effect of the estimate change to be reported in current income?

3. Prepare the adjusting entry to record bad debt expense in 2003.

© *The McGraw-Hill Companies, Inc., 2004*

Solution:

1. Neither bad debt expense nor the allowance for uncollectible accounts reported in prior years is restated. No account balances are adjusted.

2. The cumulative effect of the estimate change is not reported in current income.

3. The adjusting entry to record bad debt expense simply will reflect the new percentage. In 2003, the entry would be:

Bad debt expense (2% x $25 million)	500,000	
Allowance for uncollectible accounts		500,000

Exercise 3

At the beginning of 2000, AY Corporation purchased computer equipment for $480,000. Its useful life was estimated to be six years with no salvage value. The cost was mistakenly recorded as network maintenance expense. AY depreciates assets by the straight-line method. The error was discovered at the end of 2004, prior to adjusting and closing entries.

Required:

1. Prepare the journal entries that should have been made to record the acquisition and depreciation of the equipment. Alongside those entries prepare the entries that were incorrectly made. Determine the account balances that are incorrect as a result of the error. Ignore income taxes.

2. Prepare the journal entry to correct the error. Ignore income taxes.

Solution:

1. **Analysis:**

		Correct (Should Have Been Recorded)			Incorrect (As Recorded)	
2000	Computer equip. Cash	480,000	480,000	Expense Cash	480,000	480,000
2000	Expense Accum. deprec.	80,000	80,000	depreciation entry omitted		
2001	Expense Accum. deprec.	80,000	80,000	depreciation entry omitted		
2002	Expense Accum. deprec.	80,000	80,000	depreciation entry omitted		
2003	Expense Accum. deprec.	80,000	80,000	depreciation entry omitted		

During the four-year period, depreciation expense was *understated* by $320,000 million, but other expenses were *overstated* by $480,000, so earnings during the period was *understated* by $160,000. This means retained earnings is currently *understated* by that amount.

Accumulated depreciation is understated by $320,000. Computer equipment is understated by $480,000.

2. **To correct incorrect accounts:**

Computer equipment	480,000	
Accumulated depreciation		320,000
Retained earnings		160,000

Exercise 4
Assume the error described in Exercise 3 was not discovered until the year 2006.

Required:
Prepare the journal entry to correct the error. Ignore income taxes

Solution:

No entry would be required. After the six-year useful life the total depreciation expense would be the same as the expense incorrectly recorded at the time of purchase. So, retained earnings is no longer incorrect. Also, the asset would be fully depreciated and probably written off the books. In other words the error at this point has corrected itself. Financial statements were incorrect for six years, but now all account balances are correct.

Accounting Changes and Error Correction

MULTIPLE CHOICE

Enter the letter corresponding to the response that **best** completes each of the following statements or questions.

____ 1. Fickle Company purchased a machine at a total cost of $220,000 (no residual value) at the beginning of 2000. The machine was being depreciated over a 10-year life using the sum-of-the-years'-digits method. At the beginning of 2003, it was decided to change to straight-line. Ignoring taxes, the cumulative effect of the change in accounting principle is:
   a. $22,000
   b. $42,000
   c. $44,000
   d. $66,000

____ 2. In the previous question, the journal entry to record the cumulative effect of the change in accounting principle would include:
   a. A credit to accumulated depreciation.
   b. A debit to accumulated depreciation.
   c. A debit to retained earnings.
   d. A credit to retained earnings.

____ 3. Which of the following is not accounted for retroactively?
   a. Change in the composition of firms reporting on a consolidated basis.
   b. Change from LIFO to FIFO.
   c. Change from expensing extraordinary repairs to capitalizing the expenditures.
   d. Change from FIFO to LIFO.

____ 4. Which of the following is accounted for prospectively?
   a. Changes from SYD to DDB.
   b. Change in reporting entity.
   c. Change from the percentage-of-completion method in long-term construction.
   d. Change in the percentage used to determine bad debts.

____ 5. Early in 2003, Brandon Transport discovered that a five-year insurance premium payment of $250,000 at the beginning of 2000 was debited to insurance expense. The correcting entry would include:
   a. A debit to prepaid insurance of $250,000.
   b. A debit to insurance expense of $100,000.
   c. A debit to prepaid insurance of $150,000.
   d. A credit to retained earnings of $100,000.

_____ 6. Which of the following is not a change in accounting principle accounted for by reporting the cumulative effect of the change on the income statement?
   a. Changes from SYD to DDB.
   b. Change from FIFO to the average method.
   c. Changes from SYD to straight-line.
   d. Change from LIFO to FIFO.

_____ 7. State Materials, Inc. changed from the FIFO method of costing inventories to the weighted average method during 2003. When reported in the 2003 comparative financial statements, the 2002 inventory amount will be:
   a. Decreased.
   b. Increased.
   c. Increased or decreased, depending on how prices changed during 2003.
   d. Unaffected.

_____ 8. The current approach usually is required for:
   a. A change in estimate.
   b. A change in reporting entity.
   c. A change in accounting principle.
   d. A correction of an error.

_____ 9. Lamont Communications has amortized a patent on a straight-line basis since it was acquired in 2000 at a cost of $50 million. During 2003 management decided that the benefits from the patent would be received over a total period of 8 years rather than the 20-year legal life being used to amortize the cost. Lamont's 2003 financial statements should include:
   a. A cumulative effect adjustment of $7.5 million.
   b. Patent amortization expense of $2.5 million.
   c. Patent amortization expense of $5 million.
   d. A patent balance of $34 million.

_____ 10. Which of the following is not true regarding the correction of an error?
   a. A journal entry is made to correct any account balances that are incorrect as a result of the error.
   b. The cumulative income effect is reported net of tax on the income statement between extraordinary items and net income.
   c. Prior years' financial statements are restated to reflect the correction of the error (if the error affected those statements).
   d. A disclosure note should describe the nature of the error and the impact of its correction on net income, income before extraordinary items, and earnings per share.

____ 11. In 2003, it was discovered that Trilogy Company had debited expense for the full cost of an asset purchased on January 1, 2000. The cost was $12 million with no expected residual value. Its useful life was 5 years and straight-line depreciation is used by the company. The correcting entry assuming the error was discovered in 2003 before the adjusting and closing entries includes:
   a. A credit to accumulated depreciation of $7.2 million.
   b. A debit to accumulated depreciation of $4.8 million
   c. A credit to an asset of $12 million.
   d. A debit to retained earning of $4.8 million.

____ 12. Blair Pen Company overstated its inventory by $10 million at the end of 2003. The discovery of this error during 2004, before adjusting or closing entries, would require:
   a. A debit to inventory of $10 million.
   b. A cumulative effect adjustment in the 2004 income statement.
   c. An increase in retained earnings.
   d. None of the above.

____ 13. The discovery of the error described in the previous question in 2005, before adjusting or closing entries, would require:
   a. A credit to inventory of $10 million.
   b. A decrease in retained earnings.
   c. An increase in retained earnings.
   d. None of the above.

____ 14. Players Company changed from the sum-of-the-years'-digits method of depreciation for existing assets to the straight-line method. The cumulative effect of the change at the beginning of the period of the change should be separately reported as:
   a. A prior period adjustment.
   b. An extraordinary item.
   c. A component of income after extraordinary items.
   d. A component of income before extraordinary items.

____ 15. A change in accounting principle that should not be reported with a cumulative effect adjustment nor by restating the financial statements of prior periods is a change from the:
   a. Straight-line method of depreciating plant equipment to the declining balance method for existing equipment.
   b. Sum-of-the-years'-digits method to the straight-line method for all new equipment purchases.
   c. FIFO method to the weighted-average method.
   d. LIFO method to the weighted-average method.

___ 16. Pro forma (as if) effects of retroactive restatement usually is reported for a:
a. Change in accounting principle.
b. Change in accounting estimate.
c. Change in entity.
d. Correction of error.

___ 17. When most changes in accounting principle are made in mid-year, the cumulative effect is calculated:
a. As of the beginning of the change year.
b. As of the date of the change.
c. For the complete year applying the weighted-average approach.
d. As of the end of the change year.

___ 18. The cumulative income effect of an accounting change usually is included in earnings for the period of the change for a change in:

	Accounting Principle	Accounting Estimate
a.	Yes	Yes
b.	Yes	No
c.	No	Yes
d.	No	No

___ 19. A change in the residual value of a building depreciated on a straight-line basis is:
a. A change that should be reported in earnings of the period of change.
b. A change reported by restating prior years' financial statements.
c. An error correction.
d. A change reported in the current and future periods when the change affects both.

Answers:

1.	b.	6.	d.	11.	a.	16.	a.
2.	b.	7.	d.	12.	d.	17.	a.
3.	d.	8.	c.	13.	d.	18.	b.
4.	d.	9.	d.	14.	c.	19.	d.
5.	d.	10.	b.	15.	b.		

Statement of Cash Flows Revisited

LEARNING OBJECTIVES

After studying this chapter, you should be able to:
1. Explain the usefulness of cash flow information.
2. Describe the purpose of the statement of cash flows.
3. Relate the statement of cash flows to its historical evolution.
4. Define cash equivalents.
5. Distinguish among operating activities, investing activities, and financing activities.
6. Identify transactions that represent noncash investing and financing activities.
7. Prepare a statement of cash flows with the aid of a spreadsheet.
8. Reconcile net income to net cash flows from operating activities (the indirect method).

CHAPTER HIGHLIGHTS

The statement of cash flows is intended to help investors and creditors project their own prospective cash flows from dealings with the company. Cash flows to investors and creditors depend on the corporation generating cash flows to itself.

Purpose of the Statement

The statement reports all inflows and outflows of cash during each reporting period. Cash includes "cash equivalents" which are short-term, highly liquid investments that can readily be converted to cash with little risk of loss. This means, for example, that cash paid to buy a 3-month certificate of deposit is not considered a cash flow and is not reported on the statement of cash flows.

To make the list of cash flows more useful, the cash flows are classified according to the nature of the activities that bring about the cash flows. Specifically, the categories are cash flows from (1) operating activities, (2) investing activities, and (3) financing activities. Importantly, too, significant investing and financing activities that do not directly increase or decrease cash also are reported. These classifications are illustrated in the following example of the statement's format:

> ## Statement Format

Format Corporation
Statement of Cash Flows
For Year Ended December 31, 2003 ($ in 000s)

Cash flows from operating activities:

Cash inflows:

From customers	$230	
Cash outflows:		
To suppliers of goods	(68)	
To employees	(34)	
For interest	(10)	
For income taxes	(35)	
Net cash flows from operating activities		$83

Cash flows from investing activities:

Purchase of equipment	($45)	
Purchase of investment in stock	(32)	
Sale of land	60	
Sale of investments	15	
Net cash flows from investing activities		(2)

Cash flows from financing activities:

Issuance of bonds	$120	
Retirement of common shares	(50)	
Payment of cash dividends	(35)	
Net cash flows from financing activities		35
Net increase in cash		$116
Cash balance, January 1		75
Cash balance, December 31		$191

Noncash investing and financing activities:

Acquired $64,000 of equipment by capital lease.	$64

Cash Flows from Operating Activities

Cash flows from operating activities are both cash inflows and cash outflows that result from activities that are reported on the income statement. In effect, converting the elements of the income statement to a cash basis provides the elements of the operating activities section of the statement of cash flows. The relationship is shown below:

Accrual Basis	Cash Basis
INCOME STATEMENT	**CASH FLOWS FROM OPERATING ACTIVITIES**
Revenues:	**Cash inflows:**
Sales and service revenue	Cash received from customers
Noncash revenues and gains (e.g., gain on sale of assets)	[Not reported]
Less expenses:	**Less cash outflows:**
Cost of goods sold	Cash paid to suppliers of inventory
Salaries expense	Cash paid to employees
Noncash expenses and losses (e.g., depreciation, amortization, bad debts, loss on sale of assets)	[Not reported]
Other operating expenses	Cash paid for various expenses
Interest expense	Cash paid to banks and other creditors
Income tax expense	Cash paid to the government
Net income	**Net cash flows from operating activities**

Hint: When deciding which classification a cash flow belongs in, ask yourself first, "Is this an activity reported on the income statement?" If so, it's an operating activity. For instance, cash from interest or dividends received from investments is related to investing activities, but it is classified as an *operating activity* because investment revenue is a determinant of net income. Similarly, paying *interest* on bonds may be related to financing activities, but it is classified as an *operating activity* because interest expense is a determinant of net income.

Cash Flows from Investing Activities

Cash flows from investing activities are related to the acquisition and disposition of assets, other than (a) inventory and (b) assets classified as cash equivalents. The category includes cash paid to acquire:
> Property, plant and equipment.
> Investments in securities of other firms.
> Receivables (by making loans to others).

➡ Later transactions related to these acquisitions, such as the sale of the assets and the collection of loans, also are classified as investing activities.

Cash Flows from Financing Activities

Cash flows from financing activities result from the external financing of a business. The category includes cash received from the issuance of:
  - ➢ Common and preferred stock
  - ➢ Bonds and other debt securities

➡ Later transactions related to the sale of these securities, such as paying dividends to shareholders, the purchase of treasury stock, and the repayment of debt, also are classified as *financing activities.*

➡ Paying interest on debt is an *operating activity* because interest expense is an activity reported on the income statement.

Noncash Investing and Financing Activities

Noncash investing and financing activities include transactions such as acquiring equipment (an investing activity) by issuing a long-term note payable (a financing activity).

➡ Noncash transactions that don't affect assets or liabilities, such as the distribution of stock dividends, are **not** considered investing or financing activities and are not reported.

➡ Noncash investing and financing activities are reported either on the same page as the statement of cash flows or in a related schedule or note.

Using a Spreadsheet

A spreadsheet offers a systematic way to prepare a statement of cash flows. It allows us to analyze available data to ensure that all operating, investing, and financing activities are detected and includes automatic means of finding some errors we might make.

➡ Additionally, recording spreadsheet entries that explain account balance changes simultaneously identifies and classifies the activities to be reported on the statement of cash flows.

➡ A spreadsheet's effectiveness relies on the fact that, if cash increased or decreased, there must be a corresponding change in a *noncash* account. So, if we can identify the events and transactions that caused the change in every noncash account, we automatically will have identified all the operating, investing, and financing activities that occurred.

➡ Steps in preparing a spreadsheet:

1 On a blank spreadsheet, enter the beginning (column 1) and ending (column 4) balances of each account by transferring the comparative balance sheets and income statement. Leave

ample blank space after the balance sheets and income statement for the statement of cash flows.

2   In debit and credit columns (columns 2 and 3) enter spreadsheet entries that duplicate the actual journal entries used to record the transactions as they occurred during the year.

3   When a spreadsheet entry includes cash, enter that portion of the entry under the corresponding heading of the statement of cash flows section of the spreadsheet (that is, an operating, investing, or financing activity).

4   Because cash can't change without a corresponding change in one or more of the noncash accounts, once all noncash account balance changes are "explained" we should feel confident that we have identified all of the operating, investing, and financing activities that should be reported on the statement of cash flows.

5   A final check is to compare the change in the balance of the cash account with the net change in cash flows produced by the activities listed on the statement of cash flows section of the spreadsheet.

6   Prepare the statement of cash flows directly from the spreadsheet simply by presenting the items included in the statement of cash flows section of the spreadsheet in the appropriate format of the statement. (Be sure also to report any noncash investing and financing activities you found during the analysis.)

The Indirect Method

Either the direct or the indirect method can be used to calculate and report the net cash increase or decrease from operating activities. The direct method directly lists cash inflows and outflows. The indirect method derives cash flows *indirectly*, by starting with reported net income and "working backwards" to convert that amount to a cash basis. To illustrate, assume the following income statement and balance sheet data pertain to Format Corporation, whose statement of cash flows we looked at earlier:

INCOME STATEMENT

Sales		$250
Cost of goods sold		(70)
Gross profit		$180
Salaries expense	$35	
Depreciation expense	30	
Interest expense	12	
Loss on sale of land	6	(83)
Income before income tax expense		$ 97
Income tax expense		(39)
Net Income		$ 58

SELECTED ACCOUNTS FROM COMPARATIVE BALANCE SHEETS

Increase (decrease)

Cash	$ 7
Accounts receivable	20
Inventory	(5)
Accounts payable	(3)
Salaries payable	1
Interest payable	2
Income taxes payable	4

> **Exclude components of income that do *Not* Affect Cash Flows**

First exclude components of net income that do **not** affect cash at all. Of the seven components of net income, two – (1) depreciation expense and (2) the loss on sale of land – do **not** affect cash flows:

1. Depreciation expense is an allocation in the current period of prior cash expenditures (for assets).

2. The loss is simply the difference between cash received in the sale of land (reported as an *investing activity*) and the book value of the land. Assume, for instance, that the loss resulted from the following transaction:

Cash	29
Loss	6
Land	35

2   The cash effect of this transaction is the $29 that is reported as a cash flow from investing activities, not the $6 loss.

> **Convert to Cash the Components of Income that *Do* Affect Cash Flows**

The five other components of net income – sales, cost of goods sold, salaries, interest, and taxes – *do* affect cash flows, but not necessarily by the amount reported on the income statement.

These must be converted from the accrual basis to a cash basis. Specifically, we convert:
- ↪ Sales to cash collected from customers.
- ↪ Cost of goods sold to cash paid to suppliers.
- ↪ Salaries expense to cash paid to employees.
- ↪ Interest expense to cash paid for interest.
- ↪ Income tax expense to cash paid for taxes.

Intermediate Accounting, 3/e

The following schedule demonstrates the indirect method and allows us to compare it with the direct method of determining cash flows from operating activities:

CASH FLOWS FROM OPERATING ACTIVITIES

Income Statement		Indirect Method		Direct Method	
		Net income	$58		
		Adjustments :			
Sales	$250	Increase in A/R	(20)	Cash from customers	$230
Cost of goods sold	(70)	Decr. in inventory	5		
		Decrease in A/P	(3)	Cash to suppliers	(68)
Salaries expense	(35)	Increase in sal. pay.	1	Cash to employees	(34)
Depreciation exp.	(30)	Depreciation exp.	30	*[Not reported – no cash effect]*	
Interest exp.	(12)	Increase in int. pay.	2	Cash for interest	(10)
Loss on sale of land	(6)	Loss on sale of land	6	*[Not reported – no cash effect]*	
Income tax exp.	(39)	Increase in I.Tax/P	4	Cash paid for taxes	(35)
Net Income	**$ 58**	**Net cash flows from operating activities**	**$83**	**Net cash flows from operating activities**	**$83**

➥ Note that the indirect method yields the same net cash flows from operating activities as does the direct method.

➥ When the direct method is used, a separate schedule is required to reconcile net income with cash flows from operating activities (essentially identical to the indirect method presentation).

SELF-STUDY QUESTIONS AND EXERCISES

Concept Review

1. The statement of cash flows fills an information gap left by the balance sheet and the income statement by presenting information about _____ that the other statements either do not provide or provide only indirectly.

2. Cash includes _____ . These are short-term, highly liquid investments that can readily be converted to cash with little risk of loss.

3. Cash flows from _____ activities are both inflows and outflows of cash that result from activities reported on the income statement.

4. The payment of cash to acquire treasury stock is reported as a _____ activity in a statement of cash flows.

5. Cash flows from _____ activities are related to the acquisition and disposition of assets, other than (a) inventory and (b) assets classified as cash equivalents.

6. Cash flows from _____ activities result from the external financing of a business.

7. The net increase or decrease in cash as reported in a statement of cash flows must be reconciled on the statement with the beginning and ending cash balances from the comparative _____ .

8. Acquiring equipment by issuing a long-term note payable represents a noncash investing and financing activity reported in _____ .

9. The declaration of a _____ dividend should not be reported on a statement of cash flows.

10. A _____ provides a systematic method of preparing a statement of cash flows by analyzing available data to insure that all operating, investing, and financing activities are detected.

11. Either the _____ method or the _____ method can be used to calculate and present the net cash increase or decrease from operating activities, although the _____ method is strongly recommended by the FASB.

12. The indirect method derives cash flows *indirectly*, by starting with reported _____ and "working backwards" to convert that amount to a cash basis.

13. A(an) _____ in accounts receivable for the period means that the cash collected from customers is *more than* the reported sales amount.

14. A(an) _____ in inventory should be added to net income in deriving cash from operating activities (indirect method).

Answers:
1. cash flows **2.** cash equivalents **3.** operating **4.** financing **5.** investing **6.** financing
7. balance sheets **8.** a related disclosure schedule or note **9.** stock **10.** spreadsheet **11.** direct;
indirect; direct **12.** net income **13.** decrease **14.** decrease

REVIEW EXERCISES

Exercises 1-9 are based on the financial statements and information from the accounting records of Experimental Corporation:

Experimental Corporation
Comparative Balance Sheets
December 31, 2003 and 2002 ($ in millions)

Assets:	2003	2002
Cash	$ 55	$ 30
Accounts receivable	450	400
Prepaid insurance	15	10
Inventory	585	525
Property, plant, and equipment	790	800
Less: Accumulated depreciation	(270)	(320)
	$1,625	$1,445
Liabilities:		
Accounts payable	$ 275	$ 300
Accrued expenses payable	18	33
Bank notes payable	40	0
Bonds payable	100	0
Shareholders Equity:		
Common stock	700	700
Retained earnings	492	412
	$1,625	$1,445

Experimental Corporation
Income Statement
For the Year Ended December 31, 2003 ($ in millions)

Revenues:		
Sales revenue		$900
Expenses:		
Cost of goods sold	$400	
Depreciation expense	50	
Loss on sale of equipment	10	
Operating expenses	300	(760)
Net income		$140

Additional information from the accounting records:
a. During 2003 warehouses were purchased costing $140 million.
b. Equipment that originally cost $150 million ($\frac{2}{3}$ depreciated) sold for $40 million.
c. Experimental borrowed $40 million from its bank.
d. Consistent with its normal dividend policy, Experimental paid cash dividends of $60 million.

Exercise 1

1. Complete the T-account analysis below to determine the cash received from customers during 2003:

Accounts Receivable

Beginning balance	400 .		
Sales	_____	_____	Cash received from customers
Ending balance	450		

2. Complete the summary journal entry below to determine the cash paid to suppliers during 2003:

($ in millions)

Cash (received from customers)	
Accounts receivable	50
Sales revenue	_____

Solution:

Accounts Receivable

Beginning balance	400		
Sales	900	850	Cash received from customers
Ending balance	450		

($ in millions)

Cash (received from customers)	850
Accounts receivable	50
Sales revenue	900

Exercise 2

1. Complete the T-account analysis below to determine the cash received from customers during 2003:

Inventory

Beginning balance	525		
Goods purchased	___	___	Cost of goods sold
Ending balance	585		

Accounts Payable

		300	Beginning balance
Cash paid	___	___	Goods purchased
		275	Ending balance

2. Complete the summary journal entry below to determine the cash paid to suppliers during 2003:

($ in millions)

Cost of goods sold	
Inventory	60
Accounts payable	___
Cash (paid to suppliers of goods)	___

Solution:

Inventory

Beginning balance	525		
Goods purchased	460	400	Cost of goods sold
Ending balance	585		

Accounts Payable

		300	Beginning balance
Cash paid	485	460	Goods purchased
		275	Ending balance

($ in millions)

Cost of goods sold	400
Inventory	60
Accounts payable	25
Cash (paid to suppliers of goods)	485

Exercise 3

Complete the summary journal entry below to determine the cash paid for operating expenses during 2003:

	($ in millions)
Operating expenses	___
Prepaid insurance	___
Accrued expenses payable	___
Cash (paid for operating expenses)	___

Solution:

	($ in millions)
Operating expenses	300
Prepaid insurance	5
Accrued expenses payable	15
Cash (paid for operating expenses)	320

Exercise 4

Prepare the cash flows from operating activities section of the statement of cash flows for 2003:

Cash flows from operating activities:
Cash inflows:

$___

Cash outflows:

___

Net cash flows from operating activities $___

Solution:

Cash flows from operating activities:
Cash inflows:

From customers	$850
Cash outflows:	
To suppliers of goods	(485)
For operating expenses	(320)
Net cash flows from operating activities	$45

Exercise 5

1. Recreate the journal entry recorded when equipment was sold during 2003.

	($ in millions)
Cash (from sale of equipment)	____
Loss on sale of equipment	____
Accumulated depreciation	____
Property, plant, and equipment	____

2. Prepare the cash flows from investing activities section of the statement of cash flows for 2003:

Cash flows from investing activities:
Purchase of equipment ____
Sale of equipment ____
Net cash flows from investing activities ____

Solution:
1.

	($ in millions)
Cash (from sale of equipment)	40
Loss on sale of equipment	10
Accumulated depreciation	100
Property, plant, and equipment	150

2. **Cash flows from investing activities:**
Purchase of equipment ($140)
Sale of equipment 40
Net cash flows from investing activities (100)

Exercise 6

Prepare the cash flows from financing activities section of the statement of cash flows for 2003:

Cash flows from financing activities:
    Issuance of note payable   ___
    Issuance of bonds payable   ___
    Payment of cash dividends   ___
Net cash flows from financing activities   ___

Solution:

Cash flows from financing activities:

Issuance of note payable	$ 40
Issuance of bonds payable	100
Payment of cash dividends	(60)
Net cash flows from financing activities	80

Exercise 7

Complete the following spreadsheet for preparing a statement of cash flows for 2003:

	Dec. 31 2002	Changes Debits		Changes Credits		Dec. 31 2003
Balance Sheets						
Assets:						
Cash	30	(11)				55
Accounts receivable	400	(1)	50			450
Prepaid insurance	10	(4)				15
Inventory	525	(2)				585
Property, plant, and equipment	800	(6)	140	(7)		790
Less: Accumulated depr.	(320)	(7)		(3)		(270)
	1,445					1,625
Liabilities:						
Accounts payable	300	(2)				275
Accrued expenses payable	33	(4)				18
Notes payable	0			(8)		40
Bonds payable	0			(10)		100
Shareholders Equity:						
Common stock	700					700
Retained earnings	412	(9)		(5)		492
	1,445					1,625
Income Statement						
Revenues:						
Sales revenue				(1)	900	900
Expenses:						
Cost of goods sold		(2)				400
Depreciation expense		(3)				50
Loss on sale of equipment		(7)				10
Operating expenses		(4)				300
Net income		(5)				140
Statement of Cash Flow						
Cash flows from operating activities:						
Cash inflows:						
From customers		(1)	850			
Cash outflows:						
To suppliers of goods				(2)		
For operating expenses				(4)		
Net cash flows from operating activities						$
Cash flows from investing activities:						
Purchase of warehouses				(6)		
Sale of equipment		(7)				
Net cash flows from investing activities						
Cash flows from financing activities:						
Issuance of note payable		(8)				
Issuance of bonds payable		(10)				
Payment of cash dividends				(9)		
Net cash flows from financing activities						
Net increase in cash				(11)		
Totals			2,410		2,410	

Solution:

	Dec. 31 2002	Changes Debits		Credits		Dec. 31 2003
Balance Sheets						
Assets:						
Cash	30	(11)	25			55
Accounts receivable	400	(1)	50			450
Prepaid insurance	10	(4)	5			15
Inventory	525	(2)	60			585
Property, plant, and equipment	800	(6)	140	(7)	150	790
Less: Accumulated depr.	(320)	(7)	100	(3)	50	(270)
	1,445					1,625
Liabilities:						
Accounts payable	300	(2)	25			275
Accrued expenses payable	33	(4)	15			18
Notes payable	0			(8)	40	40
Bonds payable	0			(10)	100	100
Shareholders Equity:						
Common stock	700					700
Retained earnings	412	(9)	60	(5)	140	492
	1,445					1,625
Income Statement						
Revenues:						
Sales revenue				(1)	900	900
Expenses:						
Cost of goods sold		(2)	400			400
Depreciation expense		(3)	50			50
Loss on sale of equipment		(7)	10			10
Operating expenses		(4)	300			300
Net income		(5)	**140**			**140**
Statement of Cash Flow						
Cash flows from operating activities:						
Cash inflows:						
From customers		(1)	850			
Cash outflows:						
To suppliers of goods				(2)	485	
For operating expenses				(4)	320	
Net cash flows from operating activities						45
Cash flows from investing activities:						
Purchase of warehouses				(6)	140	
Sale of equipment		(7)	40			
Net cash flows from investing activities						(100)
Cash flows from financing activities:						
Issuance of note payable		(8)	40			
Issuance of bonds payable		(10)	100			
Payment of cash dividends				(9)	60	
Net cash flows from financing activities						80
Net increase in cash				(11)	25	25
Totals			2,410		2,410	

Exercise 8

Prepare the statement of cash flows for 2003 (direct method).

Format Corporation

Statement of Cash Flows

For Year Ended December 31, 2003 ($ in 000s)

Cash flows from operating activities:

Net cash flows from operating activities

Cash flows from investing activities:

Net cash flows from investing activities

Cash flows from financing activities:

Net cash flows from financing activities

    Net increase in cash $___

Cash balance, January 1

Cash balance, December 31 $___

Solution:

Format Corporation
Statement of Cash Flows
For Year Ended December 31, 2003 ($ in 000s)

Cash flows from operating activities:
Cash inflows:
From customers	$850	
Cash outflows:		
To suppliers of goods	(485)	
For operating expenses	(320)	
Net cash flows from operating activities		$45

Cash flows from investing activities:
Purchase of equipment	($140)	
Sale of equipment	40	
Net cash flows from investing activities		(100)

Cash flows from financing activities:
Issuance of note payable	$ 40	
Issuance of bonds payable	100	
Payment of cash dividends	(60)	
Net cash flows from financing activities		80
Net increase in cash		$25
Cash balance, January 1		30
Cash balance, December 31		$55

Exercise 9

Prepare the operating activities section of the statement of cash flows for 2003 by the indirect method. (This also is the schedule to reconcile net income and cash flows from operating activities.)

Cash flows from operating activities:

Net income		$140
Adjustments for noncash effects:		
Depreciation expense	$___	
Loss on sale of equipment	___	
Increase in accounts receivable	___	
Increase in prepaid insurance	___	
Increase in inventory	___	
Decrease in accounts payable	___	
Decrease in accrued expenses payable	___	___
Net cash flows from operating activities		$___

Solution:

Cash flows from operating activities:

Net income		$140
Adjustments for noncash effects:		
Depreciation expense	$ 50	
Loss on sale of equipment	10	
Increase in accounts receivable	(50)	
Increase in prepaid insurance	(5)	
Increase in inventory	(60)	
Decrease in accounts payable	(25)	
Decrease in accrued expenses payable	(15)	(95)
Net cash flows from operating activities		$45

MULTIPLE CHOICE

Enter the letter corresponding to the response that **best** completes each of the following statements or questions.

_____ 1. Cash equivalents have each of the following characteristics except:
   a.   Short-term.
   b.   Highly liquid.
   c.   Maturity of at least 3 months.
   d.   Little risk of loss.

_____ 2. Which of the following statements is **untrue** regarding the statement of cash flows?
   a.   The statement of cash flows presents information about cash flows that the other statements either (a) do not provide or (b) provide only indirectly.
   b.   Noncash transactions sometimes are reported also.
   c.   Either the direct or the indirect method can be used to calculate and present the net cash increase or decrease from operating activities.
   d.   The indirect method derives cash flows indirectly by starting with sales revenue and "working backwards" to convert that amount to a cash basis.

_____ 3. Stock dividends are reported in connection with a statement of cash flows as:
   a.   A financing activity.
   b.   An investing activity.
   c.   A noncash activity.
   d.   Not reported on the statement of cash flows.

_____ 4. Property dividends are reported in connection with a statement of cash flows as:
   a.   A financing activity.
   b.   An investing activity.
   c.   A noncash activity.
   d.   Not reported on the statement of cash flows.

_____ 5. Interest paid to bondholders is reported in connection with a statement of cash flows as:
   a.   An operating activity.
   b.   An investing activity.
   c.   A noncash activity.
   d.   Not reported on the statement of cash flows.

_____ 6. Investment revenue is reported in connection with a statement of cash flows as:
   a.   An operating activity.
   b.   An investing activity.
   c.   A noncash activity.
   d.   Not reported on the statement of cash flows.

_____ 7. On January 4, Henderson Corporation issued $200 million of bonds for $193 million. During the same year, $500,000 of the bond discount was amortized. On a statement of cash flows prepared by the indirect method, Henderson Corporation should report:
    a. A financing activity of $200 million.
    b. An addition to net income of $500,000.
    c. An investing activity of $193 million.
    d. A deduction from net income of $500,000.

_____ 8. Sun Company owns 14.5 million shares of stock of Center Company classified as available for sale. During 2003, the fair value of those shares increased by $19 million. What effect did this increase have on Sun's 2003 statement of cash flows?
    a. Cash from operating activities increased.
    b. Cash from investing activities increased.
    c. Cash from financing activities increased.
    d. No effect.

_____ 9. Eastern Manufacturing Company owns 40% of the outstanding common stock of Southern Supply Company. During 2003, Eastern received a $50 million cash dividend from Southern. What effect did this dividend have on Eastern's 2003 statement of cash flows?
    a. Cash from operating activities increased.
    b. Cash from investing activities increased.
    c. Cash from financing activities increased.
    d. No effect.

_____ 10. In determining cash flows from operating activities (indirect method), adjustments to net income should **not** include:
    a. An addition for depreciation expense.
    b. A deduction for bond premium amortization.
    c. An addition for a gain on sale of equipment.
    d. An addition for patent amortization.

_____ 11. The net income for World Class Corporation was $140 million for the year ended December 31, 2003. Related information follows:

    Amortization of patent, $1 million.
    Cash dividends paid, $14 million.
    Decrease in accounts receivable, $9 million
    Decrease in salaries payable, $1 million.
    Depreciation expense, $20 million.
    Increase in long-term notes payable, $13 million.
    Sale of preferred stock for cash, $17 million.

    Cash flows from operating activities during 2003 should be reported as:
    a. $151 million.
    b. $169 million.
    c. $171 million.
    d. $182 million.

____ 12. A statement of cash flows and its related disclosure note typically do not report:
   a. An acquisition of a building with a capital lease agreement.
   b. The purchase of treasury stock.
   c. Stock dividends.
   d. Notes payable issued for a tract of land.

____ 13. Sean-McDonald Company sold a printer with a cost of $34,000 and accumulated depreciation of $21,000 for $10,000 cash. This transaction would be reported as:
   a. An operating activity.
   b. An investing activity.
   c. A financing activity.
   d. None of the above.

____ 14. In a statement of cash flows (indirect method), a decrease in inventory should be reported as:
   a. A deduction from net income in determining cash flows from operating activities.
   b. An addition to net income in determining cash flows from operating activities.
   c. An investing activity.
   d. Not reported.

____ 15. In a statement of cash flows (indirect method), an increase in available-for-sale securities should be reported as:
   a. A deduction from net income in determining cash flows from operating activities.
   b. An addition to net income in determining cash flows from operating activities.
   c. An investing activity.
   d. Not reported.

____ 16. If sales revenue is $20 million and accounts receivable increased by $3 million, the amount of cash received from customers:
   a. Was $17 million.
   b. Was $20 million.
   c. Was $23 million.
   d. Depends on the proportion of cash sales and credit sales.

____ 17. If bond interest expense is $400,000, bond interest payable increased by $4,000 and bond discount decreased by $1,000, cash paid for bond interest is:
   a. $395,000.
   b. $397,000.
   c. $403,000.
   d. $405,000.

____ 18. Sales revenue for Marshall Matches was $240,000. The following data are from the accounting records of Marshall:

Bad debt expense	$2,000
Accounts receivable decrease	5,000
Allowance for uncollectible accounts increase	3,000

The cash received from customers was:
a. $235,000.
b. $244,000.
c. $245,000.
d. $246,000.

____ 19. Selected information from Mercer Corporation's accounting records and financial statements for 2003 is as follows ($ in millions):

Cash paid to acquire equipment	$18
Treasury stock purchased for cash	25
Proceeds from sale of land and buildings	45
Gain from the sale of land and buildings	26
Investment revenue received	33
Cash paid to acquire office equipment	40

On its statement of cash flows, Mercer should report net cash outflows from investing activities of:
a. $13 million.
b. $23 million.
c. $38 million.
d. $39 million.

____ 20. Selected information from Phillips Corporation's accounting records and financial statements for 2003 is as follows ($ in millions):

Cash paid to retire bonds	$30
Treasury stock purchased for cash	50
Proceeds from issuance of common stock	70
Proceeds from issuance of mortgage bonds	90
Cash dividends paid on common stock	25
Cash interest paid to bondholders	35

On its statement of cash flows, Phillips should report net cash inflows from financing activities of:
a. $20 million.
b. $55 million.
c. $70 million.
d. $105 million.

Answers:

1.	c.	6.	a.	11.	b.	16.	a.
2.	d.	7.	b.	12.	c.	17.	a.
3.	d.	8.	d.	13.	b.	18.	d.
4.	c.	9.	a.	14.	b.	19.	a.
5.	a.	10.	c.	15.	c.	20.	b.